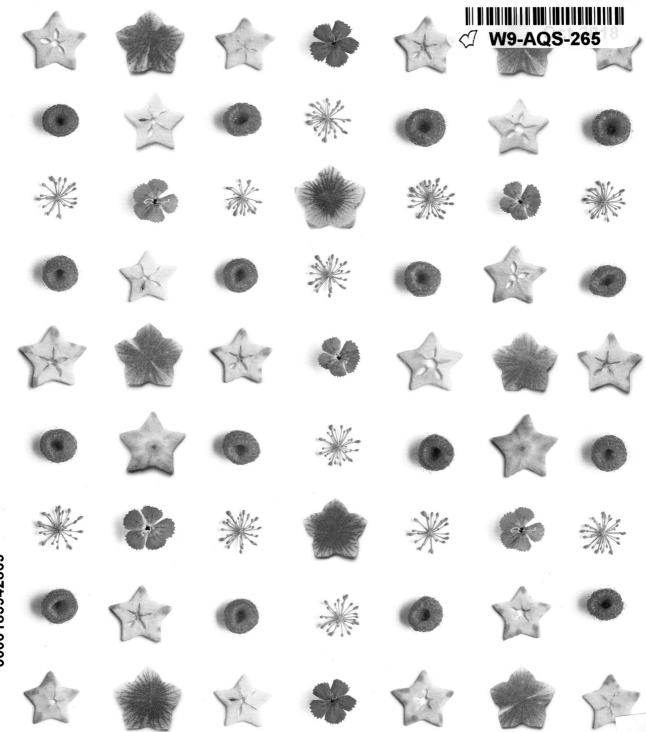

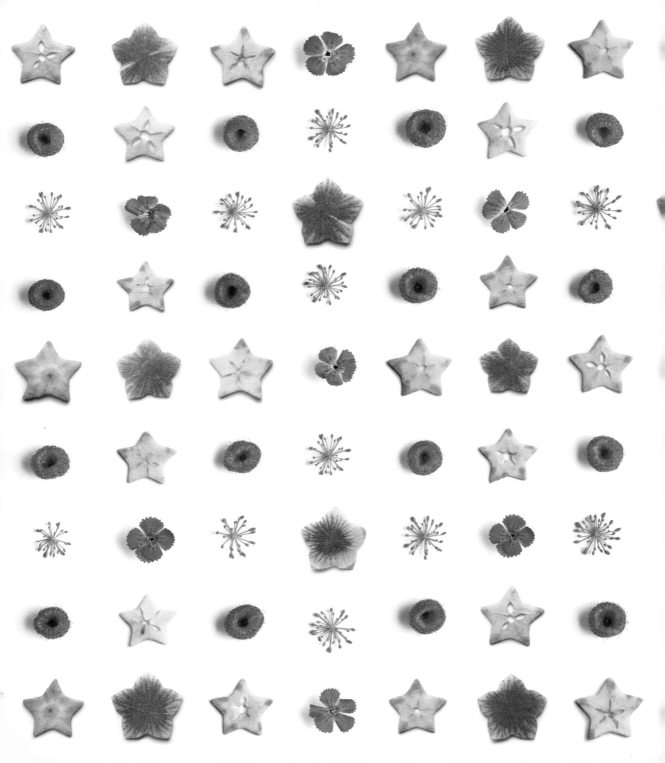

American Girl®

Garden
to
Table

Photography **Nicole Hill Gerulat**

weldon**owen**

Contents

From veggie gardens and kitchen gardens to orchards, berry patches, and citrus groves, fresh fruit and vegetables can grow everywhere!

Basil

Dill

Get Growing!

Have you ever picked a strawberry right from the patch? Imagine mixing sweet and delicious just-picked strawberries with milk and a fresh vanilla bean to create a scrumptious pudding. Big, juicy slices of watermelon are a favorite summertime treat. What if you added some of those refreshing wedges to your salad? Fresh fruits and veggies look, feel, and taste the best, and you only need a few other ingredients to transform them into super yummy meals.

This book is packed with colorful ideas for cooking and baking with fresh produce. In these pages, you'll find more than fifty recipes for awesome party foods, super fun snacks, easy dinners, and delectable desserts. Rainbow Pinwheels (page 25) are the perfect after-school snack, Mini Peach & Cherry Pies (page 91) with star and heart cutouts are really fun to bake with friends, and Mixed Berry Whipped Cream Cake (page 81) will wow guests at a Fourth of July bash. All of these irresistible dishes show off the natural flavors of just-picked ingredients. We've organized the book by when and where things grow. Play around and swap out ingredients with whatever is in season—a recipe made with peak summer veggies will offer a suggestion to make it work well in fall, for example. With these recipes as your guide, you can make everyday meals that taste fresh and exciting—and you may even discover your new favorite food. So get your garden tools ready and prepare to bring yummy seasonal fruits and veggies from the garden into your kitchen!

Be adventurous

Whether your family and friends have deemed you a cooking pro or preparing a recipe in this book is your first kitchen adventure, you'll find plenty of recipes suited to your skill level. This book is organized by where things grow—you'll find tasty recipes for summer tomatoes, zucchini, and bell peppers in Veggie Garden (pages 18–49), and tons of delicious dishes for peaches, plums, and apples in Fruit Orchard (pages 86–107). When temperatures get cooler and the first autumn winds begin to blow, transform colorful squash and hearty potatoes into meals from Harvest Time (pages 108–119). Each chapter has recipes for beginners as well as seasoned cooks, so you can choose the perfect dish for you. Before you know it, you'll be the best cook in town!

Cooking with care

 This symbol appears throughout the book to remind you that you'll need an adult to help you with all or part of the recipe. Ask for help before continuing.

Adults have lots of culinary wisdom, and they can help keep you safe in the kitchen. Always have an adult assist you, especially if your recipe involves high heat, hot ovens, deep-frying, sharp objects, and electric appliances. Be sure to wash your hands before you begin cooking and after touching raw meat, poultry, eggs, or seafood.

Top cooking tips

STAY ORGANIZED

Staying organized and paying attention are important cooking skills. Before you fire up the stove top or oven, read the recipe, including the ingredient list, from start to finish. Then it's time to clear a clean surface and lay out all your ingredients and tools. Once the food starts cooking, don't forget to set a timer!

GET HELP WITH SHARP TOOLS AND APPLIANCES

Make sure an adult helps you choose the correct knife for the task and that you're holding the handle firmly. When you're not using the knife, place it somewhere safe so it can't fall on the floor or be reached by younger siblings. Also have an adult assist you when using an electric mixer, blender, food processor, or other appliance, and keep them unplugged except when in use.

WATCH THE HEAT

Stove top burners, hot ovens, boiling water—there's a lot of heat involved in cooking, so it's important to be very careful. Always use oven mitts when handling hot equipment and have an adult help you when you're cooking at the stove top, moving things in and out of the oven, and working with hot liquids or foods.

Eat what's in season

All fruits and vegetables have a peak season when they grow in abundance and taste best. While most grow for only one season, some can be found throughout the year (such as oranges, carrots, and cauliflower). Local, seasonal foods taste better (because they're fresh) and usually cost less (because there are a lot of them available at one time). When you're shopping at the farmers' market or grocery store, buy something new each time you go, and try a different dish every week.

Spring = peas, fava beans, asparagus, rhubarb, strawberries

Summer = tomatoes, zucchini, blueberries, cherries, peaches, corn, bell peppers, melons

Fall = butternut squash, pumpkin, potatoes, apples, pears, carrots, broccoli, cauliflower

Winter = leafy greens (such as kale and chard), oranges, grapefruit, lemons, root vegetables

★ ★ ★

Grow your own

Starting a kitchen garden is easy. You can plant herbs by themselves or in clusters—just make sure they are in a sunny spot. Put pebbles around the hole in the bottom of a pot so it drains well, then fill the pot almost to the top with good potting soil and give the soil lots of water before planting. Make a hole in the soil and put in the seedling or plant, then give it a little more water. Don't forget to label your plants—then just watch them grow! All of the recipes in the Herbalicious chapter (pages 50–69) use fresh herbs, so you'll have plenty of ideas to get you started.

It's fun to find out what's in season where you live, like apples in the fall.

Veggie Garden

Great recipes start with fresh fruits and veggies that are in season, which means that they grow best at that time of year (see page 14). Spring and summer are so fun for that reason—the warm temperatures are ideal for many varieties of produce. Many recipes in this book suggest a bunch of ingredients you could use in that dish, so choose your favorite—or try something new! From hearty snacks to delicious dinners, the ideas are endless when you cook with what's growing in the garden and available at the farmers' market.

Fresh Tomato Tart

When tomatoes are in season, there is nothing better than using big, juicy slices of them as a topping for a quick and easy tart. Frozen puff pastry is the secret ingredient for whipping up this fancy-looking appetizer or lunch in a snap.

MAKES 6 TO 8 SERVINGS

All-purpose flour, for dusting

1 sheet frozen puff pastry, thawed overnight in the refrigerator

3 to 4 ripe red, orange, or yellow tomatoes, or a combination

8 to 10 red, orange, or yellow cherry tomatoes, or a combination, halved

1 recipe Herbed Goat Cheese (page 60)

 Preheat the oven to 425°F. Line a rimmed cookie sheet with parchment paper.

Very lightly dust a clean work surface with flour. Lay the puff pastry on the surface and lightly dust the top with flour. Using a rolling pin, roll out the sheet to a 10-by-15-inch rectangle about 1/8 inch thick. Place the rectangle on the prepared cookie sheet and put it in the freezer to chill while you prepare the tomatoes and herbed goat cheese.

Slice the large tomatoes into rounds. Place the tomato slices on a plate and set aside. Prepare the herbed goat cheese and set aside.

Remove the pastry from the freezer. With a sharp knife, cut a 1-inch border along the edges of the puff pastry, being careful not to cut more than halfway through the pastry. Prick the pastry inside of the border all over with a fork. Bake until the pastry is golden brown and flaky, 15 to 20 minutes. Remove from the oven and let cool on the cookie sheet on a wire rack.

Using a butter knife or the back of a spoon, spread the herbed goat cheese carefully across the pastry. Arrange the tomato slices and cherry tomato halves in overlapping rows on top. Garnish with the basil leaves remaining from making the herbed goat cheese. Cut into pieces and serve.

Veggies with Green Goddess Dip

At farmers' markets in the spring and summer, you can find veggies in a rainbow of hues. Be creative and fill this platter with all of your favorites—sugar snap peas and cherry tomatoes would also be tasty with the green goddess dip.

MAKES 4 TO 6 SERVINGS

DIP

1 cup plain Greek yogurt

1 cup watercress leaves and tender stems

2 tablespoons chopped fresh dill

1 green onion, thinly sliced

½ teaspoon sugar

½ teaspoon salt

⅛ teaspoon hot-pepper sauce such as Tabasco (optional)

6 small new or rainbow potatoes

12 small carrots, halved lengthwise

½ pound green beans

12 small assorted radishes, whole, halved, or sliced

2 small cucumbers, halved lengthwise and cut into 3-inch sticks

Fill a large saucepan about three-fourths full of water and add 1 tablespoon salt and the potatoes. Set the pan over medium-high heat and bring to a boil. Reduce the heat to medium-low and simmer, uncovered, until you can easily slide a small knife into and out of the potatoes, about 20 minutes. Drain the potatoes in a colander set in the sink. Let cool completely.

To make the dip, combine the yogurt, watercress, dill, green onion, sugar, salt, and hot-pepper sauce (if using) in a food processor or blender. Cover and process until smooth. Pour the dip into a container with a tight-fitting lid and refrigerate for several hours. The dip will be thin when first made, but it will thicken and the flavors will mellow when refrigerated. Shake or stir well before serving. The dip will keep for up to 3 days.

On a large platter, arrange the potatoes, carrots, green beans, radishes, and cucumber sticks. Put the dip in a bowl and serve right away with the veggies.

Old or new?

New potatoes are crunchy and have thin skins. They're sweeter than older potatoes because their sugars have not turned into starch yet.

Rainbow Pinwheels

These colorful rainbow roll-ups make the perfect bite-sized veggie snack, and they are great for a party. To assemble them easily, lay out the veggies and then grab a friend to help you roll them up. These are best when eaten right away.

MAKES ABOUT 18 PINWHEELS

1 carrot, peeled

1 (2-inch) piece yellow zucchini

1 (2-inch) piece cucumber, peeled

½ red bell pepper, seeded

4½ (6-inch) wholewheat, purple corn–wheat, tomato-basil, or spinach tortillas, or 1 zucchini

6 tablespoons sun-dried tomato, herb, or chive-onion cream cheese

18 small parsley or cilantro sprigs, each about 2 inches

DIP (OPTIONAL)

½ cup plain whole-milk yogurt

1 teaspoon minced fresh herbs such as chives, parsley, mint, and/or dill

Zest of ½ lemon

Cut the carrot into approximately 2-inch lengths, then cut each section lengthwise into ⅛-inch slices. Lay the slices flat and cut them lengthwise again into thin matchsticks. You should have about 36 carrot matchsticks. Place in a small bowl.

Cut the piece of zucchini lengthwise into ⅛-inch slices. Lay the slices flat and cut them lengthwise again into thin matchsticks. You should have about 36 zucchini matchsticks. Place in a second small bowl.

Cut the piece of cucumber in half lengthwise and scoop out the seeds with a small spoon. Slice each half lengthwise into thin slices. You should have about 18 cucumber matchsticks. Place in a third small bowl.

Cut the bell pepper into 2-inch-wide sections, trim away any of the ribs, then cut into thin, 2-inch-long matchsticks. You should have about 18 bell pepper matchsticks. Place in a fourth small bowl.

If using tortillas, trim about ½ inch off two opposite sides to square them up, then cut each tortilla into 4 long strips, each about 1¼ to 1½ inches wide. You will need 18 strips.

~ *Continued on page 26* ~

~ Continued from page 25 ~

Try this!
Chop up any extra veggies and toss with some lettuce and salad dressing for a quick salad.

If using zucchini, trim the ends. Using a vegetable peeler, cut the zucchini lengthwise into wide ribbons, each approximately 1 to 1½ inches wide and 5 to 6 inches long. Start on one side first; the first few ribbons will likely be too small, so discard or save for something else. Peel down to the core (stop when you see the seeds), then peel the opposite side, then the other two sides. You will need 18 strips.

To assemble the pinwheels, lay the tortilla strip or zucchini strip on a work surface. Spread about 1 teaspoon of cream cheese across the entire strip. On one end, about ½ inch in from the end, lay 2 carrot matchsticks, 2 zucchini matchsticks, 1 cucumber matchstick, 1 bell pepper matchstick, and 1 parsley sprig. Carefully roll the strip around the veggie bundle and continue rolling to the end of the strip (if the end doesn't stick, just add a little cream cheese to "glue" it together). Transfer to a platter, standing each pinwheel on its end. Continue until you finish all your veggies and tortilla or zucchini strips, transferring each to the platter after you roll it.

To make the dip (if using), stir together the yogurt, herbs, and lemon zest in a bowl. Place on the serving platter alongside the pinwheels. Serve right away.

"Cheesy" Kale Chips

You'll have to plan ahead to make these, as it takes some time to soak the cashews and dehydrate the kale chips in your oven, but almost all of it is hands-off time. And you'll be rewarded with a super delicious (and super healthy) snack.

MAKES 6 TO 8 SERVINGS

½ cup raw cashews

1 bunch curly kale (about 10 ounces)

⅓ cup nutritional yeast

2 tablespoons olive oil

1 tablespoon low-sodium soy sauce

1 tablespoon fresh lemon juice

¼ teaspoon salt

¼ teaspoon garlic powder

 Put the cashews in a bowl and add enough water to cover. Let stand for 1 hour.

Position 3 racks in the oven so that they are evenly spaced and preheat the oven to 200°F. Line 3 large rimmed cookie sheets with parchment paper. (If you don't have 3 oven racks or 3 large cookie sheets, you can use 2 and just reserve the rest of the kale in an airtight container, then bake it in batches.)

Remove the center rib from each kale leaf and discard. Tear the leaves into pieces, each about 3 inches wide. Fill a big bowl with water and add the kale, stirring it around with your hands to loosen any dirt. Drain the kale in a colander set in the sink. Repeat one or two more times until you don't see any more dirt in the water, and then dry the kale thoroughly in a salad spinner (or lay it out on paper towels and blot dry).

Drain the cashews in a fine-mesh sieve set in the sink. Combine the cashews, nutritional yeast, olive oil, soy sauce, lemon juice, salt, and garlic powder in a small food processor or a blender and process until it's a thick, rough paste.

Place the kale in a large bowl and add the cashew mixture. Using your hands, massage the cashew mixture into the kale leaves until it is evenly distributed. The paste is thick, so it will take about 5 minutes to distribute evenly; be sure to check for any hidden blobs of paste in the leaves when you are handling them.

Spread the kale leaves in a single layer, without touching, on the cookie sheets, dividing them evenly. Bake, rotating the pans to different racks every 30 minutes, until crispy, crunchy, and lightly browned, 1 hour 45 minutes to 2 hours. Be sure to check on the kale chips often toward the end of baking so they don't burn.

Remove the cookie sheets from the oven and set them atop wire racks. Let the chips cool completely. Pile onto a serving plate or in a shallow serving bowl and serve. The chips will keep in an airtight container at room temperature for up to 3 days (although they are best and most crisp the day they are made).

Hearty peppers
Meat lovers can add cooked ground beef, chicken, or turkey to the rice mixture before filling the peppers and baking them.

Stuffed Summer Bell Peppers

Colorful and hearty, these flavorful peppers have something for everyone. In summer, make use of fresh peppers, corn, and tomatoes. In winter, opt for canned tomatoes and frozen corn. If you like a little spice, swap out the jack cheese for pepper jack.

MAKES 6 SERVINGS

6 small red, orange, and/or yellow bell peppers (about 2 pounds total)

Salt

1 ear corn, shucked, or ½ cup frozen corn, thawed

2 tablespoons olive oil

¼ yellow onion, finely chopped

1 (15-ounce) can black beans, drained, rinsed, and drained again

1 large ripe tomato, cored and diced, or ½ cup canned diced tomatoes, with juices

1 tablespoon tomato paste

1 teaspoon ground cumin

1 teaspoon chili powder

(See additional ingredients, next page)

 Preheat the oven to 375°F.

To prepare the bell peppers, cut the tops off the peppers and then use a spoon to remove the seeds and ribs. Discard the tops. Rinse any remaining seeds off the peppers, and then lay the peppers out on paper towels and blot dry. Sprinkle the inside of the peppers with salt.

Arrange the peppers standing cut side up in an 8-inch baking dish. Pour ¼ cup water around the peppers, making sure no water goes into the peppers. Cover with aluminum foil and bake just until the peppers start to soften, about 15 minutes. Remove the baking dish from the oven and carefully remove the foil. Set aside.

Meanwhile, snap the ear of corn in half crosswise. Set it flat side down on a cutting board and use a paring knife to carefully cut the kernels off the cob. Set aside.

Put the oil in a large frying pan. Set the pan over medium heat. Add the onion, sprinkle with salt, and cook, stirring often, until the onion starts to soften, about 4 minutes. Stir in the beans, diced tomato with its juices, tomato paste, cumin, chili powder, 2 tablespoons water, and ½ teaspoon salt and cook until the mixture comes together and becomes fragrant, about 3 minutes.

~ *Continued on page 34* ~

Bonus rice

You'll have a cup of rice left over after stuffing the peppers, which you can add to a pot of soup or a burrito.

1 cup cooked white rice (see box)

⅔ cup shredded Monterey jack cheese

2 tablespoons minced fresh cilantro, plus more for garnish

〜 *Continued from page 33* 〜

Reduce the temperature to medium-low if it starts cooking too quickly. Stir in the corn kernels, cooked rice, and 2 tablespoons water and cook until warmed through, about 1 minute. Remove from the heat and stir in half of the cheese and the cilantro.

When the peppers are cool enough to handle, stuff them with the rice mixture, dividing it evenly. Sprinkle the tops with the rest of the cheese. Bake until the peppers are tender, the rice mixture is heated through, and the cheese is melted and starts to lightly brown, 20 to 30 minutes. Transfer each pepper to an individual plate, sprinkle with a little more cilantro, and serve right away.

How to cook rice

Place 1 cup long-grain white rice in a large fine-mesh sieve and rinse under running cold water until the water runs clear. Drain well. Transfer the rice to a medium heavy-bottomed saucepan and pour in 1½ cups water. Set the pan over medium heat and bring to a boil, stir once, and reduce the heat to low. Cover with a tight-fitting lid and cook, without removing the lid, until the rice is tender and has absorbed all the water, about 15 minutes. Turn off the heat and let sit for 5 minutes. Fluff the rice with a fork. Serve right away. (Makes 2 cups)

Broccoli & Cheddar Soup

Fresh broccoli is easy to find all year, so you can make
this creamy, hearty soup any time you're craving comfort food.
Use your favorite melty cheese, or a combo of cheeses.

MAKES 6 TO 8 SERVINGS

1½ pounds broccoli

5 cups chicken broth

**2 tablespoons
unsalted butter**

**1 yellow onion,
finely chopped**

¼ cup all-purpose flour

**1 tablespoon fresh
lemon juice**

½ teaspoon dried thyme

2 cups whole milk

**½ pound sharp Cheddar
cheese, shredded**

**Salt and ground
black pepper**

 Peel the tough broccoli stems. Coarsely chop the broccoli florets
and stems.

Pour the broth into a medium saucepan. Set the pan over high heat and
bring to a boil. Reduce the heat to medium-low to maintain a gentle simmer.

Place a large saucepan over medium heat and add the butter. When the
butter has melted, add the onion and cook, stirring often, until soft, about
8 minutes. Sprinkle in the flour and cook, stirring often, for 1 minute longer.
Add the heated broth, chopped broccoli, lemon juice, and thyme and bring
to a boil. Reduce the heat to low, cover, and simmer until the broccoli is
tender, about 20 minutes. Remove the pan from the heat and let the
broccoli mixture cool until warm, about 30 minutes.

Transfer the broccoli mixture to a blender (do this in batches if necessary).
Cover and blend until the soup is smooth. Return the soup to the saucepan,
stir in the milk, and bring to a gentle simmer over low heat. Sprinkle half
of the cheese into the soup and stir until melted. Taste the soup (careful,
it's hot!) and season with salt and pepper.

Ladle the soup into bowls and top with the rest of the cheese. Serve
right away.

Garden Veggie Minestrone

This hearty vegetarian soup makes a great meal for a crowd. Save the rind from a Parmesan cheese wedge and add it to the soup pot. It will make the broth richer and even more yummy. Use vegetable broth in place of the water to kick up the flavor.

MAKES 8 TO 10 SERVINGS

1 bunch chard or kale

1 tablespoon extra-virgin olive oil, plus more for drizzling

2 large cloves garlic, finely chopped

2 carrots, diced

1 small onion, diced

1 stalk celery, thinly sliced

Salt and ground black pepper

1 cup diced fresh or canned tomatoes, with juices

1 bay leaf

2 large fresh sage leaves

1 (2-inch) Parmesan cheese rind (optional)

2 cups drained canned cannellini beans

1 cup tubettini or other small dried pasta shape

Grated Parmesan cheese, for serving

Remove the center rib from each chard or kale leaf and discard. Tear the leaves into 3-inch pieces. Fill a big bowl with water and add the chard, stirring it around with your hands to loosen any dirt. Drain the chard in a colander set in the sink. Repeat until you don't see any more dirt in the water, and then lay it out on paper towels and blot dry.

Put 1 tablespoon oil in a large soup pot and set it over medium-high heat. Add the garlic and cook, stirring often, until the garlic is toasted, about 1 minute. Add the carrots, onion, and celery and cook, stirring often, until the vegetables start to soften and brown, 3 to 4 minutes. Season with salt and pepper.

Add the tomatoes with their juices, the bay leaf, sage, cheese rind (if using), and enough water to cover the vegetables by 2 inches and simmer, uncovered, for 30 minutes. Add the beans and chard and continue to simmer for 20 to 30 minutes more. Taste the soup (careful, it's hot!) and season with salt and pepper. Remove the cheese rind, bay leaf, and sage and discard.

Just before the soup is ready, fill a saucepan three-fourths full of water. Set the pan over high heat and bring the water to a boil. Add 1 teaspoon salt and the pasta and cook, stirring occasionally, until the pasta is al dente (tender but firm at the center); check the package directions for the cooking time. Drain the pasta in a colander set in the sink. Divide the pasta among bowls. Ladle the soup over the pasta, drizzle with oil, sprinkle generously with the grated cheese, and serve right away.

Zucchini Griddle Cakes

Zucchini grows like crazy when it's warm out. These delicious pancakes are a fun way to use up extra summer squash. Don't mix the batter until just before you are ready to cook it or the ingredients might get too mushy.

MAKES 4 TO 6 SERVINGS

4 large eggs

2 garlic cloves, minced or pushed through a garlic press

Salt and ground black pepper

½ cup all-purpose flour

1½ pounds zucchini, trimmed and coarsely grated

1 cup chopped green onions

⅓ cup fresh basil leaves, chopped

⅓ cup fresh mint leaves, chopped

1 cup feta cheese, crumbled

Extra-virgin olive oil

In a large bowl, whisk together the eggs, garlic, ½ teaspoon salt, and ½ teaspoon pepper until well blended. Whisk in the flour. With a wooden spoon or rubber spatula, stir in the zucchini, green onions, basil, and mint. Gently stir in the feta cheese.

Have a platter ready. Pour enough oil onto a griddle or into a well-seasoned cast-iron frying pan to create a thin layer. Set the griddle or pan over medium-high heat. For each cake, drop a scant ¼ cup of the batter onto the hot surface, spacing the cakes evenly. Cook until golden brown on the bottom, about 3 minutes. Slide a thin spatula under each cake, carefully flip it over, and cook until golden brown on the second side, about 3 minutes longer.

Using the spatula, transfer the cakes to a platter and loosely cover with aluminum foil to keep warm. Cook the rest of the batter in the same way, adding more oil to the pan as needed to prevent sticking. Serve right away.

Tempura String Beans

These veggie "fries" are better for you than the traditional kind, but taste just as delicious. Dip the warm beans in mayonnaise and you might never know the difference.

1 cup ice water

1 large egg, beaten

¾ cup sifted all-purpose flour, plus 2 tablespoons for dusting

3 ice cubes

Vegetable oil, for frying

1 pound green beans, trimmed

Salt

Mayonnaise, mustard, or soy sauce, for dipping (optional)

 In a bowl, whisk together the ice water and egg. Whisk in the ¾ cup flour; the batter should be quite lumpy. Add the ice cubes.

Line a large plate with paper towels and set the plate near the stove. Ask an adult to help you with frying. Pour oil to a depth of 2 inches into a heavy-bottomed saucepan or deep-fryer. Set the pan over medium heat and warm the oil until it reaches 360°F on a deep-frying thermometer.

Meanwhile, spread the beans out on a cookie sheet and dust with the 2 tablespoons flour. When the oil reaches 360°F, submerge about one-third of the beans in the batter. Use tongs to remove them from the batter 2 or 3 at a time, letting the excess drip back into the bowl, and carefully lower into the hot oil. Fry, stirring occasionally, until crisp, about 3 minutes. Use tongs to carefully remove the beans from the pot. Drain them on the paper towel–lined plate and sprinkle with salt. Cook the rest of the beans in the same way, allowing the oil to return to 360°F between batches.

If you like, serve with your choice of dip.

Spicy sauce
Kick your dip up a notch by mixing some Sriracha with the mayonnaise.

Tomato, Avocado & Bacon Tartines

Tomatoes are at their peak during the summer, especially the rainbow-colored heirlooms we use in this recipe. *Tartine* is a fancy word for open-faced sandwich, and these will look very impressive even though they are super easy to make.

MAKES 4 SERVINGS

8 thin slices bacon

4 slices country bread, each ½ inch thick

4 tablespoons mayonnaise

1 avocado, pitted, peeled, and thinly sliced

2 tomatoes, thinly sliced

Flaky sea salt

Ground black pepper (optional)

 Preheat the broiler. Line a plate with paper towels.

Lay the bacon slices in a single layer in a medium frying pan. Set the pan over medium heat and fry the bacon, turning the slices once, until golden brown and crisp, about 5 minutes. Using tongs, transfer the bacon to a paper towel-lined plate to drain.

Arrange the bread slices on a cookie sheet and put under the broiler until lightly toasted, 2 to 3 minutes. Ask an adult to help you remove the cookie sheet from the broiler.

Spread one tablespoon mayonnaise on each slice of bread and top with 2 slices of bacon, a few avocado slices, and a few tomato slices. Season with a pinch of salt and a pinch of ground black pepper (if using), and serve right away.

Pasta Primavera with Buttery Bread Crumbs

You can use any combination of colorful vegetables for this recipe. Buttery bread crumbs add crunch to the creaminess. If you like, skip the sauce and toss the pasta and veggies with extra-virgin olive oil, grated Parmesan cheese, and fresh basil.

MAKES 4 TO 6 SERVINGS

1 small green zucchini, sliced

1 small yellow zucchini, sliced

2 tablespoons olive oil

Salt and ground black pepper

2 carrots, peeled and cut diagonally into thin slices

1 tablespoon unsalted butter

1 cup dried bread crumbs

12 ounces farfalle pasta

1½ cups store-bought Alfredo sauce

1 cup cherry tomatoes, halved

Preheat the oven to 400°F. Pile the green and yellow zucchini on a rimmed cookie sheet. Drizzle with 1 tablespoon of the oil, season with salt and pepper, and toss to coat. Spread the vegetables in a single layer. Roast, stirring halfway through, until tender, about 8 minutes. Remove the cookie sheet from the oven and transfer the vegetables to a large bowl. On the same cookie sheet, toss the carrots with the remaining 1 tablespoon oil, season with salt and pepper, and spread in a single layer. Roast, stirring halfway through, until fork-tender, about 12 minutes. Remove from the oven and transfer to the bowl with the zucchini. Set aside.

Fill a large pot three-fourths full of water. Set the pot over high heat and bring the water to a boil. Meanwhile, place a frying pan over medium-high heat and add the butter. When the butter has melted, add the bread crumbs and stir to coat. Season with salt and pepper and cook, stirring often, until lightly toasted, about 2 minutes. Remove from the heat and set aside.

Heat the Alfredo sauce in a small saucepan over medium-low heat, stirring until warmed through, about 5 minutes. Remove from the heat and set aside.

Add 1 teaspoon salt and the pasta to the boiling water and cook until the pasta is al dente (tender but firm at the center); check the package directions for the cooking time. Drain the pasta and add it to the bowl with the vegetables. Stir in the Alfredo sauce and the cherry tomatoes. Taste and season with salt and pepper. Transfer to a serving dish, sprinkle with the bread crumbs, and serve.

Baked Eggplant Parmesan

Eggplant is at its best in late summer, and its firm texture holds up well when baked. Smother thick slices of this pretty purple veggie with tomato sauce and mozzarella cheese for a super satisfying summer dinner.

MAKES 4 SERVINGS

1 large egg, beaten with 1 tablespoon water

½ cup dried bread crumbs

2 tablespoons grated Parmesan cheese

½ teaspoon dried oregano

Salt and ground black pepper

2 tablespoons olive oil, plus more for oiling the dish

2 small eggplants (about 1½ pounds), trimmed and cut crosswise into 8 thick slices

2 cups jarred tomato sauce

1 cup shredded mozzarella cheese

 Preheat the oven to 400°F. Lightly oil a 9-by-13-inch baking dish.

Place the egg mixture in a wide, shallow dish. Place the bread crumbs in a second wide, shallow dish and stir in the Parmesan, oregano, ½ teaspoon salt, and ⅛ teaspoon pepper.

Put 1 tablespoon of the oil in a large frying pan. Set the pan over medium-high heat. Working with 4 eggplant slices at a time, dip a slice in the egg mixture, letting the excess drip back into the bowl. Coat both sides with the bread crumbs and carefully place in the pan. Cook, turning once, until browned, about 6 minutes. Use tongs to transfer each slice to a plate. Add the remaining oil to the pan and cook the rest of the eggplant slices in the same way.

Spoon one-third of the tomato sauce over the bottom of the prepared baking dish. Arrange 4 eggplant slices in a single layer, without touching, in the dish. Spoon one-third of the sauce onto the eggplant slices and sprinkle with half of the mozzarella. Top with the remaining 4 eggplant slices and cover with the rest of the sauce and mozzarella.

Bake until the eggplant is tender and the cheese is lightly browned and melted, about 15 minutes. Ask an adult to help you remove the baking dish from the oven. Using a wide spatula, divide among dinner plates, and serve right away.

Cheesy Cauliflower Gratin

Think of this dish as the best mac and cheese you've ever eaten, only better for you! When cauliflower cooks, it gets soft but not super mushy, so it can stand up to the ooey-gooey cheese sauce that is poured all over it.

MAKES 4 TO 6 SERVINGS

1 large head cauliflower, cut into 1-inch florets

Salt and ground black pepper

2 cups whole milk

2 tablespoons unsalted butter, plus more for greasing

2 tablespoons all-purpose flour

1 teaspoon dry mustard

½ cup shredded white Cheddar cheese

½ cup shredded Gouda cheese

Cayenne pepper (optional)

3 tablespoons dried bread crumbs

Fill a large pot three-fourths full of water. Set the pot over high heat and bring the water to a boil. Add 1 tablespoon salt and the cauliflower and cook until the florets are tender, about 7 minutes. Drain the cauliflower in a colander set in the sink and set aside.

Pour the milk into a small saucepan. Set the pan over medium heat and cook until small bubbles begin to form around the edge of the pan. Remove from the heat. Place a large saucepan over low heat and add the butter. When the butter has melted, add the flour and mustard a little at a time, whisking until blended. Raise the heat to medium-low and gradually whisk in the hot milk. Cook, stirring frequently, until the mixture is thick and creamy, about 5 minutes. Add the cheeses and a pinch of cayenne (if using). Season to taste with salt and black pepper and cook, stirring frequently, until the cheeses are melted, about 2 minutes.

Preheat the broiler and butter a shallow 2-quart gratin or baking dish. Arrange the cauliflower in the dish, pour the sauce over it, and sprinkle with the bread crumbs. Broil until golden brown, about 2 minutes. Ask an adult to help you remove the baking dish from the broiler. Serve right away.

Spring Stir-Fry with Veggies & Shrimp

Stir-frying is a quick and easy way to cook dinner. Fresh peas and asparagus are at their peak in springtime. You can also try this recipe with green beans, zucchini, snow peas, or sugar snap peas. Just remember that thicker veggies might take a little longer to cook.

MAKES 4 SERVINGS

¾ pound thin asparagus

1 tablespoon canola oil

2 garlic cloves, minced or pushed through a garlic press

1 (1-inch) piece fresh ginger, peeled and grated or minced

1 cup shelled English peas

¾ pound medium shrimp, peeled and deveined

⅓ cup low-sodium chicken or vegetable broth

1 tablespoon low-sodium soy sauce

2 cups cooked white rice (see page 34)

 Break off and discard the tough stem ends from the asparagus spears. Cut the spears on the diagonal into 1¼-inch lengths.

Put the oil in a wok or large frying pan with a lid. Set the wok over medium-high heat. Add the garlic and ginger and cook, stirring constantly, until the garlic is fragrant, about 30 seconds. Add the peas and asparagus and stir to coat with oil. Cook, stirring often, for 1 minute.

Sprinkle 3 tablespoons water into the pan. Cover and cook just until the vegetables are bright green, 1 to 2 minutes. Add the shrimp and cook, uncovered, stirring often, until opaque throughout, 2 to 3 minutes more. Add the broth and soy sauce and bring to a simmer, then immediately remove from the heat.

Serve right away with the rice on the side.

Chicken, please!
If you don't like shrimp, swap it with the same amount of chicken cut into 1-inch cubes, and cook for 3 minutes longer.

Bread-and-Butter Pickles

These sweet-and-sour pickles are really addictive, whether you eat them with burgers at a summertime barbecue or just by themselves. Pickling is much simpler than you think, and it's a great way to preserve seasonal veggies.

MAKES ABOUT 1 QUART

1 English cucumber or
6 pickling cucumbers
(about 1 pound)

1 white onion, halved
and sliced thinly into
half-moons

2 cups white
wine vinegar

¾ cup sugar

¼ cup kosher salt

1 teaspoon celery seeds

1 teaspoon mustard seeds

2 bay leaves

Have a 1-quart canning jar or other glass jar with a lid ready before you start. Cut the cucumber into slices that are about 1/4 inch thick; you should have about 4 cups. In a stainless steel or other nonreactive heatproof bowl, combine the cucumber and onion.

In a small saucepan, combine the vinegar, sugar, salt, celery seeds, mustard seeds, and bay leaves. Set the pan over high heat and bring to a boil, stirring to dissolve the sugar and salt. Remove from the heat and immediately pour the vinegar mixture over the cucumber and onion slices. Let cool to room temperature, and then pack the vegetables and liquid into the jar, discarding any excess liquid. Cover tightly and refrigerate for at least 1 hour. The pickles will keep in the refrigerator for up to 1 month.

Sweet & Spicy Melon with Lime

This is a perfect way to showcase any kind of ripe summer melon, but the ingredients may surprise you. A pinch of sea salt brings out the sweetness in the fruit, and the cayenne pepper gives it a touch of heat, but you can always leave out the cayenne.

MAKES 4 TO 6 SERVINGS

½ cup honey

¼ cup fresh lime juice, from about 2 limes

⅛ teaspoon cayenne pepper (optional)

1 teaspoon grated lime zest

1 mini seedless watermelon (about 3 pounds)

1 small ripe cantaloupe (about 3 pounds)

Sea salt

2 to 3 tablespoons torn fresh mint leaves

Combine the honey, lime juice, and cayenne (if using), in a small saucepan. Set the pan over medium-high heat and bring to a boil, then reduce the heat to low and simmer for 3 minutes to blend the flavors. Remove from the heat and let cool to lukewarm. Stir in the lime zest. Let cool to room temperature.

Cut the rind from the watermelon, and then cut the flesh into bite-sized cubes. Halve the cantaloupe. Scoop out the seeds and discard. Cut off the rind, and then cut the flesh into cubes.

Place all of the melon in a wide, shallow serving bowl and drizzle with half of the honey-lime syrup. Toss gently to coat, then drizzle with the rest of the syrup. Sprinkle with a pinch of salt and the mint and serve right away.

Herbalicious

You don't need a big backyard to get growing—
you can start in your very own kitchen! Adding
fresh herbs boosts the flavor of any dish, and
growing your own is easier than you think.
Did you know that you can eat flowers?
Well, you can! Edible flowers include pansies,
nasturtiums, marigolds, violets, and geraniums,
and they're perfect for decorating cakes,
cupcakes, and even tea sandwiches! Learn
how to create an indoor kitchen herb and flower
garden on page 14, and find out how much
fun it is to watch everything grow.

Tomato, Watermelon & Mint Salad

Heirloom varieties of produce go back for generations and are known for their rich flavor and interesting colors and shapes. The tomatoes come in almost every color of the rainbow, so use your favorite combination for this sweet summer salad.

MAKES 6 SERVINGS

1 mini seedless watermelon (about 3 pounds)

1¾ pounds heirloom tomatoes, sliced

2 Persian cucumbers, thinly sliced crosswise or shaved into ribbons with a vegetable peeler

2 tablespoons extra-virgin olive oil

2 tablespoons white wine vinegar

3 ounces feta cheese, crumbled

½ cup fresh mint leaves

Salt and ground black pepper

 Cut the rind from the watermelon. Cut the flesh into 3-inch wedges, and then thinly slice the wedges.

In a large shallow serving bowl, arrange the watermelon, tomatoes, and cucumbers. Drizzle the oil and vinegar over the mixture, sprinkle with feta, mint, a pinch each of salt and pepper, and serve right away.

Tool-tastic!
Use a vegetable peeler to "shave" veggies, such as cucumber and zucchini, into long ribbons—your meals will look even prettier.

Cashew Chicken Lettuce Cups

This playful spin on tacos starts with a savory Asian-style chicken and vegetable stir-fry, then uses crisp, fresh lettuce as a stand-in for tortillas. Chopped cashews add crunch and cilantro adds freshness. If you don't like spicy food, leave out the jalapeño.

MAKES 4 SERVINGS

2 heads little gem lettuce or romaine lettuce hearts

¾ pound skinless, boneless chicken breast halves

1 medium green bell pepper

1 large red bell pepper

¼ cup low-sodium chicken broth

2 tablespoons hoisin sauce

1 tablespoon low-sodium soy sauce

1 teaspoon rice vinegar

¼ teaspoon sesame oil

1 tablespoon cornstarch

2 tablespoons canola oil

3 cloves garlic, minced

4 green onions, sliced

1 jalapeño chile, thinly sliced (optional)

½ cup coarsely chopped raw cashews

Coarsely chopped fresh cilantro (optional)

Using your fingers, separate the lettuce leaves from the lettuce heads, tearing out any tough ribs and discarding any blemished or discolored leaves. Pile the leaves onto a serving plate, cover with moist paper towels, and refrigerate.

Cut the chicken into ½-inch cubes. Seed and dice the green and red bell peppers.

In a small bowl, whisk together the chicken broth, hoisin sauce, soy sauce, vinegar, sesame oil, and cornstarch. Set aside.

Put the canola oil in a wok or large nonstick frying pan. Set the pan over medium-high heat. When the oil is almost smoking, add the chicken and cook, stirring and tossing constantly, until browned, 1 to 2 minutes. Using a slotted spoon, transfer the chicken to a plate. Add the bell peppers, garlic, green onions, and jalapeño (if using), to the pan and cook, stirring and tossing constantly, until tender-crisp, about 2 minutes. Return the chicken to the pan and add the cashews. Whisk the soy sauce mixture to recombine, add to the pan, and cook, stirring and tossing constantly, until the chicken is opaque throughout and the sauce is nicely thickened, 2 to 3 minutes longer.

Spoon the chicken-vegetable mixture onto the lettuce leaves and add cilantro (if using). Place on a platter and serve right away.

Tea Sandwiches

These dainty open-faced sandwiches are easy to make but oh so pretty! We freshened up whipped cream cheese with herbs from the garden (use any combination you like) then topped each bread slice with a mix of cucumbers, radishes, herbs, and edible flowers.

MAKES 4 SERVINGS

1 (4-ounce) container whipped cream cheese

½ teaspoon minced fresh chives

½ teaspoon minced fresh dill or basil

½ teaspoon grated lemon zest

6 small, thin slices good-quality whole-wheat or white sandwich bread, cut on the diagonal to form 12 triangles, crusts removed, or 12 slices baguette, cut on the diagonal

1 Persian cucumber, thinly sliced

4 radishes, thinly sliced crosswise

Garnishes (see box)

In a bowl, stir together the cream cheese, chives, dill, and lemon zest. Dollop heaping teaspoonfuls of the cream cheese mixture onto each slice of bread, then spread in a thick layer to the edges of the bread. Top each with a few slices of either cucumber or radish. Arrange on a platter.

Garnish each piece of bread with snipped pieces of herbs or a pinch of arugula or microgreens, and an edible flower or two. Serve right away.

Tea sandwich garnishes

Microgreens are simply baby versions of arugula or other edible immature salad greens that are picked when they first sprout in the garden; look for them at farmers' markets.

¼ cup mixed fresh herbs, such as 1-inch pieces of chive, small mint or basil leaves, or little sprigs of dill

¼ cup baby arugula or microgreens

¼ cup edible flowers such as pansies, nasturtiums, rose petals, mini roses, marigolds, violets, Sweet Williams, and/or geraniums

Fresh Herb Panzanella

Originally from Tuscany, Italy, panzanella is salad made with day-old bread and tomatoes. The stale bread softens when it soaks up the oil, vinegar, and tomato juices. Garden-fresh herbs add a touch of tanginess.

MAKES 6 SERVINGS

½ pound country bread, thickly sliced

1 large clove garlic, peeled and halved

2 pounds heirloom tomatoes (see page 53)

2 small Persian cucumbers

½ red onion, thinly sliced

6 tablespoons extra-virgin olive oil

2 tablespoons red wine vinegar

2 tablespoons capers

Salt and ground black pepper

1½ cups arugula, torn

3 tablespoons fresh basil leaves, torn

2 tablespoons fresh oregano leaves

1 (2-ounce) wedge Parmesan cheese

 Preheat the oven to 375°F. Arrange the bread slices on a rimmed cookie sheet. Toast in the oven, turning once, until golden brown, about 5 minutes. Remove the cookie sheet from the oven. Let cool slightly, then rub the bread slices on both sides with the garlic clove.

Core and thinly slice the tomatoes. Halve the cucumbers lengthwise, then thinly slice crosswise into half-moons.

In a large serving bowl, combine the tomatoes, cucumbers, onion, oil, vinegar, capers, and ½ teaspoon salt. With your hands, tear the bread into 1-inch pieces and add to the bowl. Stir to combine and let stand until the bread is soft and soaked with tomato juices, about 10 minutes.

Add the arugula, basil, and oregano to the salad and toss to combine. Season with pepper. Using a vegetable peeler, shave thin pieces from the wedge of cheese over the salad. Serve right away.

Make it a meal
Add grilled chicken slices to this salad for a hearty lunch or summertime dinner.

Chopped Caesar Salad

Did you know you can regrow romaine lettuce indoors? Place its "heart" (the bottom) in a shallow dish of water on a windowsill near light, and change the water every few days. After about 10 days, it will regrow new leaves. Trim any outer leaves that turn brown.

MAKES 4 SERVINGS

DRESSING

1 cup olive oil

¼ cup mayonnaise

4 garlic cloves, chopped

2 tablespoons plus
2 teaspoons Dijon
mustard

Juice of 3 lemons

1 tablespoon plus
1 teaspoon
Worcestershire sauce

Salt and ground
black pepper

6 cups romaine lettuce
leaves, coarsely chopped

2 cups cooked chicken,
sliced or shredded
(optional)

1 (2-ounce) wedge
Parmesan cheese

1 cup store-bought
croutons

 To make the dressing, combine the oil, mayonnaise, garlic, Dijon mustard, lemon juice, Worcestershire sauce, 1 tablespoon plus 1 teaspoon salt, and ¼ teaspoon pepper in a blender. Cover and blend until smooth. Set aside ½ cup and transfer any remaining dressing to a sealed jar; it will keep in the fridge for up to 5 days.

Put the lettuce in a large container with a tight-fitting lid and add ½ cup of the dressing. Cover the container tightly and toss gently until the lettuce is evenly coated with the dressing.

Transfer the lettuce to a large serving plate and top with the chicken (if using). Using a vegetable peeler, shave thin pieces from the wedge of cheese over the salad. Sprinkle with pepper to taste. Top with the croutons and serve right away.

Vegetable & Herbed Goat Cheese Bruschetta

You can change up this dish throughout the year depending on what's in season. Try it with roasted beets or cubes of butternut squash in the winter; asparagus or mashed fava beans are perfect in spring; eggplant is a great option in the summer.

MAKES 4 SERVINGS

4 asparagus spears, cut into 1-inch strips

2 red bell peppers, seeded and cut into 1-inch strips

2 portobello mushrooms, sliced

1 zucchini, cut into ¼-inch rounds

¼ cup plus 1 tablespoon extra-virgin olive oil

2 tablespoons red wine vinegar

Salt and ground black pepper

4 slices country bread, each ½ inch thick

HERBED GOAT CHEESE

¼ pound goat cheese, at room temperature

2 tablespoons chopped fresh basil, plus small basil leaves for serving

2 tablespoons chopped fresh parsley

3 tablespoons heavy cream

 In a medium bowl, toss the asparagus, bell peppers, mushrooms, and zucchini with ¼ cup oil and the vinegar. Season well with salt and pepper, toss again, and set aside.

Warm a grill pan or frying pan over high heat. Brush both sides of the bread with the remaining 1 tablespoon oil and place on the grill pan. Cook until nicely grill-marked on both sides, 2 to 3 minutes per side. Transfer to a plate.

Working in batches to avoid crowding, place the vegetables in the grill pan and cook until nicely grill-marked, about 3 minutes per side for the zucchini, 4 minutes per side for the mushrooms, and 5 minutes per side for the bell peppers. Transfer the vegetables to another plate as they're done and let cool slightly.

To make the herbed goat cheese, stir together the goat cheese, chopped basil, parsley, and cream in a small bowl. Season with salt and pepper. Dollop heaping teaspoonfuls of the herbed goat cheese onto each slice of grilled bread, then spread in a thick layer to the edges of the bread. Arrange on a platter.

Top each piece of bread with grilled vegetables and a few basil leaves. Serve right away, passing extra vegetables at the table.

Eat these blooms
Not only are they pretty, but some flowers are even edible. See our list on page 57 and choose your favorites for decorating this cake.

Flower Sandwich Cake

This beautiful layer cake has a big surprise—it's really a savory sandwich! Layers of flatbread, cream cheese, cucumbers, and smoked salmon are decorated with herbs and veggies—there is nothing cuter for a summertime lunch fresh from the garden.

MAKES 6 TO 8 SERVINGS

5 flat gyro pita wraps or thick, soft white pita bread, each 6½ to 7 inches in diameter and ¼ inch thick

2 (8-ounce) containers whipped cream cheese

¼ cup plus ⅓ cup fromage blanc (or fresh farmer cheese)

1 teaspoon minced fresh dill, plus dill fronds for decorating

1 teaspoon minced fresh chives, plus 1 bunch for decorating

1 teaspoon fresh lemon juice

½ large cucumber (about 5 ounces), very thinly sliced

4 ounces thinly sliced smoked salmon

1 or 2 small radishes, cut into quarters

Edible flowers, for decorating

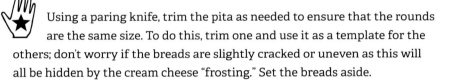

Using a paring knife, trim the pita as needed to ensure that the rounds are the same size. To do this, trim one and use it as a template for the others; don't worry if the breads are slightly cracked or uneven as this will all be hidden by the cream cheese "frosting." Set the breads aside.

To make the filling, in a bowl, stir together 1 container cream cheese, ¼ cup fromage blanc, 1 teaspoon minced dill, 1 teaspoon minced chives, and the lemon juice until well combined.

Place one bread onto a flat round serving plate or platter. Using a small offset spatula or a mini rubber spatula, spread ¼ of the cream cheese filling (about ¼ cup) in an even layer over the top of the bread. Top with half of the cucumber slices, placing them in an even layer and overlapping them in a decorative pattern. Top with a second bread, then spread ¼ cup of the cream cheese filling onto the bread. Top with half of the salmon, placing the slices in an even layer. Top with a third bread, ¼ cup cream cheese filling, and the remaining cucumber slices. Top with a fourth bread, the remaining cream cheese filling, and the remaining salmon slices. Top with the final bread and press the "cake" gently to make sure the top is even.

~ *Continued on page 64* ~

Say cheese!
Fromage *is the French word for cheese. Fromage blanc is a creamy white soft French cheese made from cow's milk that spreads easily.*

~ *Continued from page 63* ~

In a bowl, combine the remaining container cream cheese and ⅓ cup fromage blanc and stir vigorously until the mixture is smooth. Using a small offset spatula or a mini rubber spatula, spread the "frosting" all over the sides and top of the cake, making sure to fill in the gaps on the sides of the cake and covering the cake in an even layer.

To decorate, cut the 1 bunch chives into 3-to-4-inch-long pieces. Press the chives into the sides of the cake one by one so that they stick to the "frosting" and resemble grass. Top the cake with the radish pieces, edible flowers, and dill fronds. Cut into wedges and serve right away, or loosely cover with plastic wrap and refrigerate for up to 4 hours before serving.

Hodgepodge with Herbs & Polenta

Put the produce from a summer garden to use in this boldly flavored vegetarian meal. Use a mix of hearty fresh herbs, such as basil, oregano, and thyme—you can even try growing your own (see page 14). The sauce is also good tossed with pasta and olive oil.

MAKES 6 SERVINGS

1 recipe cooked Polenta (see box)

2 tablespoons extra-virgin olive oil

1 small yellow onion, chopped

1 red, yellow, or orange bell pepper, seeded and sliced

1 large green chile such as Anaheim, Hatch, or poblano, seeded and sliced

Salt

1½ pounds tomatoes, cored and chopped

¼ cup plus 2 tablespoons chopped fresh herbs such as thyme, basil, oregano, and/or marjoram

4 cloves garlic, chopped

2 zucchini or crookneck squash, trimmed and sliced into ¼-inch rounds

1 cup cherry tomatoes

Grated Parmesan cheese, for serving

While the polenta is cooking (see box), make the hodgepodge. Put the oil in a large, heavy frying pan. Set the pan over medium heat. Add the onion, bell pepper, chile, and a pinch of salt and cook, stirring often, until tender, about 12 minutes. Add the tomatoes and cook, stirring often, until tender, 7 to 8 minutes. Stir in ¼ cup of the herbs and the garlic and cook, stirring, for 1 minute. Add the zucchini and cherry tomatoes, cover, and cook until the zucchini is tender and the cherry tomatoes have burst, about 5 minutes.

Divide the polenta among bowls. Spoon the hodgepodge over the polenta, dividing it evenly, and sprinkle with the remaining 2 tablespoons herbs and the Parmesan cheese. Serve right away.

How to cook polenta

Fill a saucepan with 4 cups water. Add 2 tablespoons unsalted butter and 1 teaspoon salt, set the pan over high heat, and bring to a boil. Add 1 cup coarse-ground polenta or yellow cornmeal in a thin, steady stream while whisking constantly. Reduce the heat to medium and continue to whisk for 1 minute. Reduce the heat to low, cover, and cook, stirring occasionally, until thick and creamy, about 40 minutes. Remove it from the heat, stir in ½ cup grated Parmesan cheese, and season with black pepper. Serve right away or cover and leave at room temperature for up to 20 minutes.

Basil

Fruity cubes
Pour your favorite colorful fruit juices into a square or star-shaped silicone ice cube mold. Freeze until firm.

Fruit, Herb & Flower Ice Cubes

These special little ice cubes will wow your friends and family. We used sprigs of herbs, colorful edible flowers, and a mixture of berries to create these little works of art. You can also try star-shaped ice cube molds and fill them with multicolored fruit juices.

MAKES 25 ICE CUBES

1½ quarts distilled water

Fresh herbs such as mint leaves, or rosemary sprigs, or chive blossoms

Edible flowers such as pansies, nasturtiums, rose petals, mini roses, marigolds, violets, Sweet Williams, and/or geraniums

Berries such as blueberries and/or raspberries

Fill a saucepan with the distilled water. Set the pan over high heat and bring to a boil. Remove from the heat and set aside to cool completely. (Distilled water has fewer impurities than tap water, and boiling it creates clear, rather than cloudy, ice cubes.)

Gather as many herb leaves or sprigs, flowers, or berries as you have ice cube molds. Make sure your herb sprigs, flowers, or petals are clean and dry. Use 2 or more berries per cube depending on how big they are. Place the berries in an even layer on a small tray and freeze until solid before using.

Fill each ice cube mold with some of the cooled distilled water so it comes about a third of the way up the mold. Place an herb sprig, a flower, or a few berries into each cube, alternating some facedown and some faceup (they might shift as they freeze). Place in the freezer and freeze until firm. Put the rest of the distilled water in the refrigerator while the cubes set.

Remove the tray from the freezer and add a little more water, filling each mold again about a third of the way (don't be tempted to overfill it or it will melt and the herb, flower, or berry will float). Gently push the herb, flower, or berry down if it floats. Put the tray back in the freezer and freeze the next layer until firm. Top off each ice cube mold with water to fill it to the top. Return to the freezer and freeze until firm. You can keep the ice cubes in the mold or remove and put them in a bowl and then use the molds to make more.

Berry Patch

When strawberries, blueberries, raspberries, blackberries, and other berries are in season, you're in for a real treat. They are so sweet and delicious that you don't need lots of other ingredients to create a show-stopping dessert or refreshing drink. Play around with the varieties that you cook and bake with, or use a combination of a few. Visit a strawberry patch in the spring or early summer to pick your own beautiful berries— they'll taste and look so pretty that you'll want to make every recipe in this chapter!

Strawberry Cupcakes

A triple dose of strawberries—in the cupcakes, frosting, and decorations—will make strawberry lovers really happy. If you want to punch up the pink color, add a few drops of red food coloring to the batter or buttercream.

MAKES 12 CUPCAKES

CUPCAKES

2 tablespoons strawberry jam

¼ cup finely chopped strawberries, plus 12 whole strawberries for garnish

1¼ cups all-purpose flour

1¼ teaspoons baking powder

¼ teaspoon salt

¾ cup granulated sugar

½ cup (1 stick) unsalted butter, at room temperature

3 large egg whites, at room temperature

½ teaspoon pure vanilla extract

4 drops red food coloring (optional)

⅓ cup whole milk

(See additional ingredients, next page)

 Preheat the oven to 350°F. Line a standard 12-cup muffin pan with paper or foil liners.

To make the cupcakes, in a small bowl, stir together the jam and chopped strawberries.

In a medium bowl, whisk together the flour, baking powder, and salt. In a large bowl, using an electric mixer, beat the granulated sugar and butter on medium-high speed until fluffy and pale, 2 to 3 minutes. Add the egg whites, vanilla, and red food coloring (if using), and beat until combined. Turn off the mixer and scrape down the bowl with a rubber spatula. Add about a third of the flour mixture and beat on low speed until just combined. Beat in half of the milk. Turn off the mixer. Add another third of the flour mixture and beat until just combined. Beat in the rest of the milk. Turn off the mixer. Add the rest of the flour mixture and beat until just combined. Fold in the strawberry jam mixture until just combined.

Divide the batter evenly among the prepared muffin cups, filling each about three-fourths full. Bake until lightly golden and a wooden skewer inserted in the center of a cupcake comes out clean, about 25 minutes. Remove the muffin pan from the oven and set it atop a wire rack. Let cool for 5 minutes, then carefully transfer the cupcakes directly to the rack. Let cool completely.

~ Continued on page 74 ~

Cupcakes for days!
Refrigerate frosted cupcakes in an airtight container for up to 3 days. Bring to room temperature before serving.

~ *Continued from page 73* ~

While the cupcakes cool, make the frosting. In the bowl of a stand mixer fitted with the paddle attachment, or in a large bowl using an electric mixer, beat the butter on medium-high speed until fluffy and pale, about 2 minutes. Add half of the powdered sugar and beat until just combined. Add the vanilla and beat until smooth, about 1 minute. Turn off the mixer and scrape down the bowl with a rubber spatula. Add the cream and beat until thick and creamy, about 3 minutes. Turn off the mixer. Add the jam and red food coloring (if using), and beat until combined.

Using a small icing spatula or a butter knife, frost the cupcakes. Top each with a fresh strawberry and serve right away.

FROSTING

1 cup (2 sticks)
unsalted butter,
at room temperature

6 cups powdered sugar

1 tablespoon pure
vanilla extract

¼ cup heavy cream

⅓ to ⅔ cup
strawberry jam

6 drops red food
coloring (optional)

Strawberry Puddings

Chocolate pudding will always be awesome, but these sweet strawberry treats are delicious in spring and summer, when fresh berries are at their peak. Serve them in small, pretty glasses so you can see the fruit nestled inside.

MAKES 4 TO 6 PUDDINGS

3 teaspoons powdered gelatin

1 cup whole milk

¾ cup powdered sugar

1 vanilla bean, split lengthwise

2½ cups buttermilk

2 cups strawberries, hulled and diced

 Pour ¼ cup water into a small bowl, sprinkle with the gelatin, and stir to combine. Let stand for 5 minutes to soften.

Combine the milk, powdered sugar, and vanilla bean in a saucepan. Set the pan over medium heat and bring to a simmer, stirring to dissolve the sugar. Simmer for 5 minutes, then add the gelatin mixture and stir until dissolved. Remove from the heat and let cool slightly. When the milk mixture has cooled, remove the vanilla bean and discard. Add the buttermilk and 1 cup of the strawberries to the milk mixture and stir until combined.

Divide the strawberry mixture evenly among 4 to 6 small glasses, filling them to about ½ inch below the rim. Cover the glasses with plastic wrap and refrigerate until the puddings are set, at least 3 hours or up to 2 days. The rest of the strawberries will keep in an airtight container for up to 2 days.

When ready to serve, spoon the chilled strawberries over the puddings, dividing them evenly. Serve cold.

Blackberry Slab Pie

Slab pie really is a genius dessert. It has all the elements of a traditional round pie—a flaky crust bursting with fresh fruit—but will feed a crowd, is easier to make, and is less fussy to serve. You can use any type of berry, but blackberries are always a favorite.

MAKES 8 TO 10 SERVINGS

All-purpose flour, for dusting

1 package (2 sheets) store-bought pie dough, divided into 2 disks

4 pints blackberries

1 cup sugar

¼ cup instant tapioca

2 teaspoons grated lemon zest

½ teaspoon ground cinnamon

¼ teaspoon ground allspice

¼ teaspoon salt

3 tablespoons unsalted butter, cut into small pieces

1 large egg, beaten with 1 teaspoon water

Place a rack in the lower third of the oven and preheat to 375°F.

Very lightly dust a clean work surface with flour. Lay the pie dough on the surface and lightly dust the top with flour. Using a rolling pin, roll out 1 dough disk into an 11-by-14-inch rectangle. Transfer to a 9-by-12 inch rimmed cookie sheet and fit the dough into the bottom and up the sides of the pan. Roll out the other dough disk on a piece of parchment paper into another 11-by-14-inch rectangle.

In a large bowl, gently stir together the blackberries, sugar, tapioca, lemon zest, cinnamon, allspice, and salt. Pour the filling into the crust in the pan and spread to the edges of the crust. Sprinkle the butter pieces over the top.

Using the parchment, turn the rolled-out crust upside down and lower it onto the filling, lining up the edges. Peel off the parchment. Trim the dough edges, leaving 3/4 inch of the dough extending past the sides of the cookie sheet. Fold the extra dough under itself and use your fingers to crimp the edges together.

Lightly brush the dough with the egg mixture. Using a paring knife, make about twelve 1-inch slashes in the top crust to create steam vents.

Bake until the crust is golden brown and the filling is bubbling, 45 to 50 minutes, covering the crust with aluminum foil if it browns too quickly. Remove the cookie sheet from the oven and set it atop a wire rack. Let cool completely before serving, at least 2 hours. Cut into squares and serve.

Mixed Berry Whipped Cream Cake

Pound cake is very versatile and pairs well with so many ingredients. Any combination of berries will work for this cake, such as blackberries and raspberries. When rhubarb is in season, top the cake with ice cream and Rhubarb-Raspberry Sauce (see variation).

MAKES 8 SERVINGS

CAKE

2 cups all-purpose flour

½ teaspoon baking powder

¼ teaspoon salt

1 cup (2 sticks) unsalted butter, at room temperature, plus more for greasing the pan

1½ cups granulated sugar

4 large eggs, beaten

1 teaspoon pure vanilla extract

¼ cup heavy cream

FILLING

1 cup cold heavy cream

¼ cup powdered sugar, plus more for dusting

1 teaspoon pure vanilla extract

1 cup raspberries

1 cup blueberries

1 cup strawberries

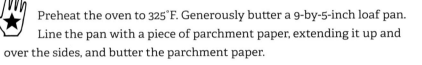

Preheat the oven to 325°F. Generously butter a 9-by-5-inch loaf pan. Line the pan with a piece of parchment paper, extending it up and over the sides, and butter the parchment paper.

To make the cake, sift together the flour, baking powder, and salt into a bowl. In a large bowl, using an electric mixer, beat the butter and granulated sugar on medium speed until fluffy and pale, about 2 minutes. Add the eggs, 1 at a time, beating well after each addition. Mix in the vanilla. Turn off the mixer and scrape down the bowl with a rubber spatula. Add half of the flour mixture and mix on low speed just until blended. Turn off the mixer. Pour in the cream and mix on low speed just until combined. Turn off the mixer. Add the rest of the flour mixture and mix just until a smooth batter forms.

Pour the batter into the prepared pan. Bake until the top of the cake is golden and a wooden skewer inserted into the center comes out clean, about 1 hour.

Remove the pan from the oven and set atop a wire rack. Let the cake cool in the pan for about 20 minutes, then, using the parchment, carefully lift the cake out of the pan, remove the parchment, and place the cake on the rack. Let cool.

To make the filling, in a large bowl, using an electric mixer, beat the cream, powdered sugar, and vanilla on medium-high speed until stiff peaks form, 3 to 4 minutes.

~ *Continued on page 82* ~

Special sundae

Top a slice of pound cake with a big scoop of ice cream, hot fudge, whipped cream, and sprinkles for the ultimate treat.

~ *Continued from page 81* ~

Cut the cake horizontally into 3 equal layers with a serrated knife. Place the bottom cake layer on a serving plate and, using a small offset spatula or mini rubber spatula, spread with half of the whipped cream. Top with a layer of berries. Place the middle cake layer on top and spread with the rest of the whipped cream. Top with another layer of berries. Top with the final cake layer.

Refrigerate for at least 2 hours or up to 5 hours. Just before serving, put some powdered sugar into a fine-mesh sieve, hold the sieve over the cake, and tap the side of the sieve to dust the cake with sugar. Cut into thick slices and serve right away.

Variation: Rhubarb-Raspberry Sauce

Combine 2 large stalks rhubarb (about 1 pound), 1 cup raspberries, ⅓ cup sugar, and ¼ cup water in a heavy-bottomed saucepan. Set the pan over medium heat and cook, stirring occasionally, until the rhubarb is soft, about 10 minutes. Remove from the heat and let cool slightly. Put a slice of pound cake onto a dish, place a scoop of vanilla ice cream on top, and drizzle with the rhubarb-raspberry sauce.

Three-Berry Cobbler

Berries are a natural fit for an ooey-gooey cobbler, but you can also mix and match other in-season fruit and choose a jam accordingly. Try peaches, plums, or cherries with apricot jam since they are all stone fruits. Tapioca helps to thicken the filling.

MAKES 6 SERVINGS

FILLING

2 pints raspberries

2 pints strawberries, hulled and halved lengthwise

1 pint blueberries

¼ cup raspberry jam

1 tablespoon instant tapioca

TOPPING

½ cup whole wheat flour

½ cup all-purpose flour

2 teaspoons baking powder

½ teaspoon salt

¼ teaspoon baking soda

3 tablespoons unsalted butter, at room temperature, plus more for greasing the pan

⅓ cup sugar

⅓ cup buttermilk

 Preheat the oven to 350°F. Grease an 8-inch square metal baking pan or ceramic baking dish lightly with butter. (Do not use a glass dish.)

To make the filling, in a bowl, combine the raspberries, strawberries, blueberries, jam, and tapioca. Using a rubber spatula, stir gently to coat the berries with the jam. Spread the fruit in an even layer in the prepared pan.

To make the topping, in a second bowl, whisk together the flours, baking powder, salt, and baking soda. In a third bowl, using an electric mixer, beat the butter and sugar on high speed until fluffy and pale, about 3 minutes. Reduce the speed to medium and beat in about half of the buttermilk. Turn off the mixer and scrape down the bowl with a rubber spatula. Add about half of the dry ingredients and beat until almost combined. Beat in the rest of the buttermilk. Turn off the mixer. Add the rest of the dry ingredients and beat until a thick, sticky batter forms. Do not overmix.

Use an ice cream scoop to drop heaping spoonfuls of the batter over the fruit. Spread it as evenly as possible, using the back of the spoon. It's okay if some of the fruit shows through.

Bake the cobbler until the crust is deep golden brown and the fruit juices bubble up around the edges, about 40 minutes. Remove the baking pan from the oven and set it atop a wire rack. Let cool to lukewarm before serving. Scoop the cobbler onto dessert plates and serve right away.

Fresh Fruit Spa Water

Adding fresh fruit to a jug of cold water imbues it with sweet perfume. Experiment with colors, like purply-blue blackberries, marionberries, and blueberries, or green honeydew melon pieces, sliced cucumber, and fresh mint. Or mix it all up and create rainbow water!

MAKES 8 SERVINGS

1 red-skinned apple such as Pink Lady

½ pound strawberries, hulled and sliced

3 ounces raspberries

Juice of ½ lemon

 Cut the apple into quarters, and then cut out the core with a paring knife. Cut the apple lengthwise into thin slices. Combine the apple, strawberries, raspberries, and lemon juice in a clear 3-quart (or larger) pitcher. Fill with 2 quarts cold water, then add ice to chill. Serve right away or refrigerate for up to 1 day (replace the ice when you serve).

Fruit Orchard

So many delicious types of fruit grow on trees—
from juicy peaches, plums, and cherries in the
summer to crisp, refreshing apples and pears
in the fall. You can make everything from salsa
to ice cream with them, and their firm yet juicy
texture makes them an ideal ingredient for
baking as well. A weekend trip to the apple
orchard is the perfect way to welcome fall and
is a fun place to pick a bounty of goodies for
snacking and cooking with throughout the week.
Preserve their flavor well into winter by making a
big batch of homemade applesauce (page 107).

Fresh Peach Salsa

Salsa can be made with more than just tomatoes. When peaches or avocados are in season, try one of these fun and yummy versions with a big bowl of tortilla chips. Chiles lend an authentic flavor, but you can leave them out if they are too spicy for your taste.

MAKES 4 TO 6 SERVINGS

2 peaches, diced

3 tablespoons diced red onion

3 tablespoons chopped fresh cilantro

½ to 1½ teaspoons minced canned chipotle chile in adobo sauce (optional)

1 teaspoon fresh lime juice

Salt and ground black pepper

 In a medium bowl, combine the peaches, red onion, cilantro, chile (if using), and lime juice.

Season to taste with salt and black pepper. Cover and let stand at room temperature for at least 30 minutes or up to 3 hours.

Variation: Avocado Salsa

In a medium bowl, combine ¼ cup finely chopped white onion, 2 large diced plum tomatoes, half of a finely chopped serrano chile, ¼ cup minced fresh cilantro, and 3 tablespoons fresh lime juice. Gently mix in 1 diced avocado. Season to taste with salt and ground black pepper. Cover and let stand at room temperature for at least 30 minutes or up to 3 hours.

Try this!
Salsa is always great for dipping, but these chunky varieties are also awesome as a topping for grilled chicken or fish.

Mini Peach & Cherry Pies

Choose peaches or nectarines that are fragrant and at the peak of ripeness. They should give just slightly when gently pressed. Rock-hard stone fruit isn't as sweet, and really ripe fruits should be eaten fresh with the juices running down your chin.

MAKES 8 MINI PIES

All-purpose flour,
for dusting

1 package (2 sheets)
frozen store-bought pie
dough, divided into 2 disks

1 to 1¼ pounds firm, ripe
peaches or nectarines
(about 3), or 2 cups pitted
cherries (see page 93),
halved, or a combination
of ½ pound peaches and
1 cup cherries

¼ cup granulated sugar

1 tablespoon
tapioca flour

1 teaspoon fresh
lemon juice

1 large egg, beaten with
1 teaspoon water

1 tablespoon raw sugar,
for sprinkling

Coat a standard 12-cup muffin pan with nonstick cooking spray. Very lightly dust a clean work surface with flour. Lay the pie dough on the surface and thaw for about 10 minutes. When the dough is pliable, using a 4¼-inch round cookie or biscuit cutter, cut out 4 rounds from each piece of dough, making sure you leave some room to cut out shapes for topping the pies. You should have a total of 8 rounds. Press each round gently into a muffin cup. Refrigerate the muffin pan.

Coat a small cookie sheet lightly with cooking spray. Use a star- and/or heart-shaped cookie cutter to cut out 8 shapes from the remaining dough that are just big enough to cover the tops of the muffin cups (about 2½ inches across). (If you don't have a star- or heart-shaped cutter, you can use any shape that will fit across the muffin cup.) Place the shapes on the cookie sheet and freeze until ready to bake.

If using peaches or nectarines, fill a large saucepan three-fourths full of water. Set the pan over high heat and bring the water to a boil. Gently lower the peaches into the boiling water with a slotted spoon. Let boil for 30 seconds, then remove with the slotted spoon and transfer to a clean work surface. When they are cool enough to handle, slip off the skins, using your fingertips or a paring knife (ask an adult for help). Using a paring knife, make a cut all the way around the peach, from stem end to blossom end and back.

~ Continued on page 92 ~

Perfect pastry

We used all-butter frozen pie dough, but you can always make your own. Roll it out to ⅛ inch thick before cutting it into shapes.

~ *Continued from page 91* ~

Gently twist the fruit to separate the two halves and remove the pit. Cut each peach half into ¼- to ½-inch slices, then cut the slices into ½-inch pieces.

Preheat the oven to 375°F.

In a bowl, stir together the peaches (and/or cherries), granulated sugar, tapioca flour, and lemon juice until well combined. Remove the chilled pie shells from the refrigerator and divide the filling among the shells. Remove the cookie sheet with the cutout shapes from the freezer and brush each shape with the egg mixture (you will not use all of it). Sprinkle with the raw sugar.

Bake the cutouts and pies until the cutouts are golden brown and the pies are bubbly and golden brown, about 15 minutes for the cutouts and 25 to 30 minutes for the pies. Remove the cookie sheet with the cutouts from the oven and set it atop a wire rack to cool. Remove the pies from the oven and set atop a second wire rack. Place a cutout atop each pie. Let the pies cool until warm, then use a small offset spatula or butter knife to gently remove them from the pan (you may need to run the spatula or knife around the edge to loosen it). Serve warm or at room temperature.

Cherry Juice Sparkler

In cherry season, the markets are spilling over with all varieties and colors. Bing cherries have a rich, dark flesh and a deep flavor, making them perfect for juicing, but you can use any kind you like.

MAKES 2 SERVINGS

3 cups Bing cherries, plus ¼ cup more for garnish

Crushed ice or ice cubes

½ liter sparkling water

Stem the cherries. Using a cherry pitter, pit the cherries. Discard the pits. Purée the cherries in a blender. Pass the mixture through a sieve to strain out the juice. (You can use the reserved cherry pieces for fruit salad or oatmeal.)

Fill two tall glasses with crushed ice and pour in the juice, dividing it evenly. Top with sparkling water, garnish with whole cherries, and serve right away.

Variation: Berry Juice Sparkler

Try making this refreshing drink with fresh strawberries, raspberries, blueberries, or blackberries. Purée 3 cups of any combination of berries in a blender. Pass the mixture through a sieve to strain out the juice. Fill two tall glasses with crushed ice and pour in the juice, dividing it evenly. Top with ½ liter sparkling water, garnish with fresh berries, and serve right away.

Peach Ice Cream

Dozens of peach varieties are available in the summer, from small and white to oversize and orange-hued. You'll need an ice cream maker for this recipe, and you can leave the peach skins on because they add lovely color and pure peach flavor.

MAKES ABOUT 1 QUART

**1 pound peaches,
pitted and chopped**

1 cup sugar

½ teaspoon citric acid

1¼ cups heavy cream

6 large egg yolks

**1 teaspoon pure
vanilla extract**

 In a large bowl, combine the peaches, ½ cup of the sugar, and the citric acid. Stir and mash the peaches gently with the back of a spoon.

Pour the cream into a heavy saucepan. Set the pan over medium heat and bring to a gentle boil. In a second large bowl, whisk together the egg yolks and the remaining ½ cup sugar until blended. Remove the cream from the heat and gradually whisk it into the egg mixture. Return the mixture to the pan and cook over low heat, stirring constantly, until the custard thickens enough to coat the back of the spoon, about 8 minutes. Do not boil. Strain the custard through a fine-mesh sieve set over a bowl and let cool until just warm.

Whisk the custard into the peach mixture, then stir in the vanilla. Transfer the custard to an ice cream maker and freeze according to the manufacturer's directions. Serve right away, or store in an airtight container in the freezer for up to 2 weeks.

Peachy keen

Citric acid keeps cut peaches from turning brown when oxygen from the air hits them. You can buy it at cake-supply stores.

Little Plum Galettes

Think of these cute desserts as individual fruit pies. Use plums or pluots (a plum-apricot hybrid), or a combo of both. When folding the dough into pleats, work quickly so your fingers don't melt the butter in the dough, which could toughen the crust.

MAKES 8 GALETTES

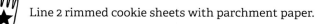

All-purose flour, for dusting

1 package (2 sheets) store-bought pie dough, divided into 2 disks

½ cup granulated sugar

2 tablespoons cornstarch

¼ teaspoon ground cinnamon

⅛ teaspoon salt

2 pounds plums or pluots, pitted and sliced ¼ inch thick (about 4 cups)

1 large egg, beaten with 1 teaspoon water

1 tablespoon raw sugar, for sprinkling

Line 2 rimmed cookie sheets with parchment paper.

Very lightly dust a clean work surface with flour. Lay the pie dough on the surface and lightly dust the top with flour. Using a rolling pin, roll out both dough disks into 12-inch rounds. Using a 6-inch round cookie cutter (or a 6-inch cardboard circle and a small sharp knife), cut out 3 or 4 rounds from each piece of dough. Press the scraps together and reroll to cut out more rounds. You should have a total of 8 rounds. Place the dough rounds on the prepared cookie sheets. Do not trim the edges of the dough.

In a small bowl, stir together the granulated sugar, cornstarch, cinnamon, and salt. Place the plums in a large bowl, sprinkle with the sugar mixture, and toss.

Place about ½ cup of the plum mixture in the center of each dough round, leaving a 1-inch border uncovered all around. Fold the border up and over the filling of each tart, forming loose pleats all around the edges and leaving the centers open, with the plums uncovered. Refrigerate the galettes on the cookie sheets until the dough is firm, 15 to 20 minutes.

Meanwhile, place a rack in the lower third of the oven and preheat to 350°F. Lightly brush the top crusts with the egg mixture (you will not use all of it) and sprinkle with raw sugar. Bake until the crusts are golden and the juice around the plums has thickened, about 40 minutes. Remove the cookie sheets from the oven and set them atop wire racks. Let cool slightly before serving.

Baked Nectarines with Cinnamon Streusel

Streusel is a crumbly mixture of flour, sugar, butter, nuts, and spices that is used as a topping for cakes and muffins—and fruit! You can use peaches, plums, or pluots instead of the nectarines for this recipe, and a scoop of vanilla ice cream on top is always a hit.

MAKES 4 SERVINGS

4 firm, ripe nectarines, halved and pitted

¼ cup plus 2 tablespoons whole wheat flour

¼ cup plus 2 tablespoons firmly packed light brown sugar

½ teaspoon ground cinnamon

⅛ teaspoon salt

2 tablespoons cold unsalted butter, cut into small pieces

⅓ cup roasted almonds, chopped

 Preheat the oven to 400°F. Line a rimmed cookie sheet with parchment paper.

Arrange the nectarines, cut side up, on the prepared cookie sheet. Cut a thin slice off the round side of each half to help them sit flat, if you like. Set aside.

In a food processor, combine the flour, brown sugar, cinnamon, and salt and pulse a few times to mix. Scatter the butter pieces over the flour mixture and pulse just until the mixture resembles coarse crumbs. Do not overmix. Transfer to a bowl and stir in the almonds. Squeeze the flour-sugar-butter mixture into small handfuls and scatter it evenly over the nectarine halves, pressing it lightly so that it sticks to the nectarines.

Bake until the nectarines are tender when pierced with a small knife and the topping is nicely browned, about 20 minutes. Arrange 2 nectarine halves on each of 4 dessert plates and serve right away.

Frosted Apple Cake

This cake is great for an after-school snack or big get-togethers. You can use a variety of apples, such as McIntosh, Fuji, pippin, or Granny Smith. We used a combo of thinly sliced rings of green Granny Smith and red Gravenstein apples for the garnish.

MAKES 12 SERVINGS

CAKE

2 cups all-purpose flour

1 teaspoon baking powder

1 teaspoon baking soda

1 teaspoon ground cinnamon

½ teaspoon ground nutmeg

½ teaspoon ground cloves

½ teaspoon salt

¾ cup (1½ sticks) unsalted butter, at room temperature

1½ cups granulated sugar

3 large eggs, at room temperature

½ cup buttermilk, at room temperature

2 cups peeled diced apples (from about 3 apples)

½ cup walnuts, toasted and chopped (optional)

(See additional ingredients, next page)

Preheat the oven to 350°F. Line a 9-by-13-inch baking pan with a piece of parchment paper, extending it up and over the short sides.

To make the cake, sift together the flour, baking powder, baking soda, cinnamon, nutmeg, cloves, and salt onto a sheet of parchment paper. In a large bowl, using an electric mixer, beat the butter and granulated sugar on medium-high speed until fluffy and pale, 3 to 5 minutes. Add the eggs, 1 at a time, beating well after each addition. Turn off the mixer and scrape down the bowl with a rubber spatula.

Using the spatula, gently fold in about a third of the flour mixture. Stir in half of the buttermilk. Add another third of the flour mixture and fold just until combined. Stir in the rest of the buttermilk, then add the rest of the flour mixture and fold just until combined. Fold in the apples and the walnuts (if using). Do not fold too vigorously or the cake will be tough. Pour the batter into the prepared pan and spread the top evenly.

Bake until the top is brown and a wooden skewer inserted into the center of the cake comes out clean, 35 to 40 minutes. Ask an adult to help you remove the baking pan from the oven and set it atop a wire rack. Let cool completely.

~ Continued on page 104 ~

Packable snack
Skip the frosting
(it can get messy) and
wrap up pieces of this
cake to enjoy after lunch
or after school.

~ *Continued from page 103* ~

While the cake cools, make the cream cheese frosting. In a large bowl, using an electric mixer, beat the cream cheese and butter on medium-high speed until smooth, 3 to 5 minutes. Reduce the speed to low, add the powdered sugar, and beat until smooth, about 2 minutes. Beat in the vanilla. Turn off the mixer and scrape down the bowl with a rubber spatula.

When the cake is cool, using the parchment, carefully lift the cake out. Remove the parchment and place the cake on a tray or platter. Using a long offset spatula, spread the frosting over the top of the cake. Arrange the apple slices in overlapping rows across the top. Cut the cake into squares and serve right away.

FROSTING

2 (8-ounce) packages
cream cheese,
at room temperature

6 tablespoons
unsalted butter,
at room temperature

1¼ cups powdered sugar

1½ teaspoons pure
vanilla extract

Thin apple slices,
for garnish

Inside-Out Apple Crisp

The next time you go apple picking with friends, set aside a few pretty apples for this quick and easy dessert. If you're feeding a crowd, double or triple this recipe and serve the apples with vanilla yogurt, whipped cream, or ice cream.

MAKES 4 SERVINGS

4 large baking apples such as Fuji or Golden Delicious

½ cup rolled oats

¾ cup firmly packed light brown sugar

1 teaspoon ground cinnamon

¼ teaspoon ground nutmeg

¼ teaspoon salt

½ cup (1 stick) cold unsalted butter, cut into small pieces

½ cup apple juice

 Using an apple corer, core the apples and set aside.

In a small bowl, stir together the oats, brown sugar, cinnamon, nutmeg, and salt until well mixed. Scatter the butter pieces over the oat mixture, and using your fingertips, rub the butter into the sugar-oat mixture until the mixture holds together in small chunks.

Stuff the oat mixture into the cored center of each apple, dividing it evenly. Stand the apples upright in an 8-inch square baking pan. Pour the apple juice into the bottom of the pan.

Bake until golden and tender when pierced with a knife, about 35 minutes. Remove the baking pan from the oven. Transfer the apples to individual serving bowls and serve right away.

Chunky Applesauce

Homemade applesauce is super simple to make, and it's the perfect way to welcome fall. Bring some to school for lunch or a snack, use it as a substitute for oil when baking, or pour fresh-from-the-stove sauce over ice cream for dessert.

MAKES 4 TO 6 SERVINGS

4 Fuji or Braeburn apples

¼ cup sugar

2 teaspoons fresh lemon juice

Salt

Peel the apples, cut into quarters, and then cut out the cores with a paring knife. Cut the apple quarters into chunks. You should have about 4 cups diced apples. Place in a saucepan, add the sugar, ¼ cup water, lemon juice, and a pinch of salt, and stir well. Set the pan over medium-high heat and bring to a boil. Immediately reduce the heat to low, cover, and simmer until tender, about 30 minutes. If the apples begin to dry out before they are ready, add a little more water.

Uncover the pan and mash the apples lightly with a wooden spoon or a rubber spatula. Continue to cook for 5 minutes longer to evaporate some of the excess moisture. The applesauce should be thick. Remove from the heat and serve warm or chilled. Store leftovers in an airtight container in the refrigerator for up to 3 days.

Mix and match
Use a mix of 2 pears and 2 apples, or use all pears. You can also scent the sauce with a pinch of ground cinnamon.

Harvest Time

When warm summer nights give way to cool fall days, the fruits and vegetables that grow outside change too. Hearty pumpkins, squash, and potatoes in a beautiful mix of orange, yellow, and green hues are everywhere, and the cooler climate is ideal for firing up the oven. Try roasting a colorful combination of root vegetables tossed with maple syrup (page 110), or topping your favorite pasta shape with sweet butternut squash and crispy bacon (page 113). We've collected a bunch of fun ideas for cooking with the fall bounty, so we're sure you'll find a favorite.

Maple-Glazed Roasted Root Vegetables

Tossing fall veggies with maple syrup gives them a caramel-like flavor after they are roasted. Use any combo of the ones listed here, or try mixing in some pieces of fresh pumpkin—and don't be shy about doubling up on your favorites.

MAKES 4 TO 6 SERVINGS

2 carrots, cut into 2-inch pieces

1 large parsnip, cut into 2-inch pieces

1 small turnip, cut into chunks

½ rutabaga, cut into chunks

1 sweet potato, peeled and cut into chunks

2 or 3 beets, peeled and cut into chunks

1 red onion, cut into chunks

3 tablespoons olive oil

2 teaspoons salt

2 tablespoons unsalted butter

¼ cup pure maple syrup

 Preheat the oven to 400°F.

In a large bowl, combine the carrots, parsnip, turnip, rutabaga, sweet potato, beets, and onion. Pour in the oil and toss to coat. Season with the salt and toss again. Spread the vegetables in a single layer on 2 rimmed cookie sheets.

Roast, shaking the cookie sheets occasionally and turning the vegetables with a spatula to keep them from sticking, until they develop a light crust and are tender, 40 to 50 minutes.

Meanwhile, place a small saucepan over medium heat and add the butter. When the butter has melted, add the maple syrup and stir to combine. Ask an adult to help you remove the cookie sheets from the oven, and then brush the maple syrup mixture over the vegetables.

Continue roasting the vegetables until they look glazed, about 5 minutes longer. Remove the cookie sheets from the oven and transfer the vegetables to a serving dish. Serve right away.

Chef's trick

Pasta water absorbs starch from noodles when they cook, so adding a little to your sauce will help bind all of the ingredients together.

Pasta with Butternut Squash & Bacon

The sweet roasted squash—a perfect match for salty bacon—breaks down a little when it is tossed with the pasta, making the sauce taste really creamy and oh so delish. This pretty dish is hearty and warming, especially on a chilly fall night.

MAKES 4 SERVINGS

1 butternut squash, about 1½ pounds, halved lengthwise, seeded, peeled, and cut into bite-sized cubes

½ cup diced yellow onion

1 tablespoon extra-virgin olive oil

Salt and ground black pepper

3 tablespoons unsalted butter

½ pound gemelli, fusilli, penne, or orecchiette pasta

4 slices thick-cut bacon, chopped

1 tablespoon fresh sage

½ cup grated Parmesan cheese

Preheat the oven to 400°F. Pile the squash and onion on a rimmed cookie sheet. Drizzle with oil, season with salt and pepper, and toss to coat. Spread the vegetables in a single layer. Cut 1 tablespoon of the butter into bits and scatter over the squash. Roast, rotating the pan halfway through cooking, until the squash and onion are golden and tender, about 45 minutes. Ask an adult to help remove the cookie sheet from the oven and set aside.

Bring a large pot three-fourths full of water. Set the pot over high heat and bring the water to a boil. Add 1 teaspoon salt and the pasta and cook until the pasta is al dente (tender but firm at the center); check the package directions for the cooking time. Turn off the heat and scoop 1 cup of the pasta cooking water out of the pot and set aside. Drain the pasta and set aside.

While the pasta is cooking, set a large sauté pan over medium heat. Add the bacon and cook, stirring often, until the bacon is crisp on the edges but still chewy at the center, 4 to 5 minutes. Ask an adult to help you pour off all but 1 tablespoon fat from the pan, and then return the pan to medium-high heat. Add the sage and cook, stirring often, for 30 seconds. Add the roasted squash mixture and cook, stirring occasionally, until heated through, about 2 minutes.

Add the pasta, remaining 2 tablespoons butter, and ¼ cup of the pasta water and stir. If the pasta seems dry, stir in a little more pasta water. Season to taste with salt and pepper. Transfer to a serving dish, add the cheese, and serve.

Sweet Potato Skins with Cheese & Spinach

Sweet potatoes are a delicious and healthy alternative to regular white potatoes. In this super yummy recipe, they are baked twice and stuffed with spinach, provolone cheese, and spiced pecans.

MAKES 4 SERVINGS

4 large sweet potatoes (each about ¾ pound), scrubbed well

1 cup grated provolone or Cheddar cheese

2 tablespoons white miso

2 teaspoons extra-virgin olive oil

4 cups packed baby spinach leaves

Salt and ground black pepper

2 tablespoons unsalted butter

1 cup pecans, coarsely chopped

4 teaspoons firmly packed light brown sugar

2 teaspoons chopped fresh rosemary

⅛ teaspoon cayenne pepper (optional)

Preheat the oven to 350°F. Prick the sweet potatoes all over with a fork. Place the sweet potatoes on a cookie sheet and bake until tender, 45 minutes to 1 hour. Remove the cookie sheet from the oven and set aside to cool slightly. (Or, after pricking them, place the sweet potatoes on a paper towel and microwave on high, turning once or twice, for 10 to 15 minutes.)

When the sweet potatoes are cool enough to handle, use a paring knife to cut a long slit down the length of them. Using a sturdy spoon, scoop out the centers, leaving the skin and about ½ inch of flesh intact. Transfer the scooped-out flesh to a large bowl. Add the cheese and miso to the bowl, and use a potato masher or fork to mash until mostly smooth and well combined.

Put the oil in a sauté pan. Set the pan over medium heat. Add the spinach and cook, stirring often, until wilted, about 3 minutes. Transfer the spinach to the bowl with the mashed sweet potatoes and stir to combine; season to taste with salt and black pepper. Spoon the mixture into the sweet potato skins.

Place a small saucepan over medium heat and add the butter. When the butter has melted, pour it into a small bowl. Add the pecans, brown sugar, rosemary, cayenne (if using), ½ teaspoon salt, and ¼ teaspoon black pepper and stir to combine. Sprinkle the nut mixture on top of the stuffed sweet potatoes. Place the sweet potatoes on the same cookie sheet and bake until the tops are golden brown, about 25 minutes. Remove the cookie sheet from the oven and let the sweet potatoes cool for a few minutes. Serve right away.

Roasted Potatoes with Herbs

Believe it or not, potatoes have seasons too. Waxy potatoes have a thin skin, sweet flavor, and creamy texture, and are at their peak in the spring and early summer. They are ideal for roasting because they hold their shape when cooked for awhile in a hot oven.

MAKES 4 TO 6 SERVINGS

¼ cup olive oil

2 tablespoons fresh lemon juice

¼ teaspoon paprika

Salt and ground black pepper

2½ pounds unpeeled waxy potatoes, such as Yukon Gold, scrubbed well and cut into 2-inch pieces

1 tablespoon chopped fresh basil

1 tablespoon chopped fresh chives

 Preheat the oven to 425°F.

In a small bowl, stir together the oil, lemon juice, paprika, 1 teaspoon salt, and ½ teaspoon pepper.

Pile the potatoes in a roasting pan. Drizzle with the oil mixture and toss to coat. Spread the potatoes in a single layer, without touching. Roast, turning the potatoes with a spatula to keep them from sticking, until golden brown, about 45 minutes. Ask an adult to help remove the pan from the oven and transfer to a serving dish. Sprinkle with basil and chives. Serve right away.

Little spuds
If using smaller "new" potatoes, you can roast them whole.

Acorn Squash & Chorizo Tart

Frozen puff pastry is fun and easy to cook with. This savory tart is ideal for fall when acorn squash is in season, but you can use a combo of zucchini and feta cheese or tomatoes and goat cheese when those veggies are at their peak in the summer.

MAKES 8 SERVINGS

All-purpose flour,
for dusting

1 sheet frozen puff
pastry, thawed overnight
in the refrigerator

½ pound acorn squash,
seeded and cut into
½-inch slices

2 tablespoons olive oil

¼ teaspoon salt

¼ pound Spanish-style
chorizo, diced

½ cup shredded
Monterey jack cheese

½ red onion, thinly sliced

1 large egg, beaten with
1 teaspoon water

Place a rack in the bottom third of the oven and preheat it to 400°F. Line a rimmed cookie sheet with parchment paper.

Lightly dust a clean work surface with flour. Lay the puff pastry on the surface and lightly dust the top with flour. Using a rolling pin, roll out the sheet to a 10-by-15-inch rectangle about 1/8 inch thick. Place the rectangle on the prepared cookie sheet and put it in the freezer while you prepare the squash.

Line a second rimmed cookie sheet with parchment paper. Pile the squash on the prepared cookie sheet, drizzle with 1 tablespoon of the oil, season with the salt, and toss to coat. Spread the squash in a single layer. Roast until almost tender, about 10 minutes. Remove the cookie sheet from the oven.

Line a plate with paper towels. Put the remaining 1 tablespoon oil in a large frying pan. Set the pan over medium-high heat. Add the chorizo and cook, stirring often, until lightly browned, about 2 minutes. Using a slotted spoon, carefully transfer the chorizo to the paper towel-lined plate to drain.

Remove the pastry from the freezer. Sprinkle the cheese evenly across the top, leaving a 1½-inch border uncovered around the edges. Place the onion slices evenly on top of the cheese. Arrange the squash slices in slightly overlapping rows inside the border, then scatter the chorizo pieces on top of the squash. Lightly brush the pastry border with the egg mixture. Bake until the crust is golden brown, about 30 minutes. Cut into rectangles and serve right away.

Citrus Grove

Lemons, oranges, grapefruit, and other citrus fruits are usually available year-round, so you can make the recipes in this chapter all year long. When they are at their peak during the winter, make fresh-squeezed orange juice or a sparkling limeade (page 134). In the summer, cool off with frozen grapefruit granita (page 135) or tangy, creamy ice pops swirled with strawberry (page 127). If you've never eaten a blood orange, try using one to make a delicious cake topped with a yummy pink icing made from the blood orange juice.

Orangey Quinoa Bowl with Veggies

Quinoa is a protein-packed grain, making it a hearty and filling alternative to rice. A mix of veggies and a refreshing vinaigrette add lots of color and flavor to this one-bowl meal. Ricotta salata, an aged ricotta, is a salty, crumbly cheese. If you can't find it, use feta instead.

MAKES 4 SERVINGS

1½ pounds small carrots, peeled and cut in half lengthwise

3 tablespoons olive oil

Salt and ground black pepper

1 cup quinoa

3 oranges or blood oranges

10 ounces baby spinach leaves

¾ cup shelled edamame, fresh or frozen and cooked

⅓ cup toasted hazelnuts, chopped

5 ounces ricotta salata or feta cheese

VINAIGRETTE

Juice of 2 oranges

2 tablespoons red wine vinegar

2 teaspoons Dijon mustard

¼ cup olive oil

Salt and ground black pepper

Preheat the oven to 400°F. Line a rimmed cookie sheet with parchment paper. Pile the carrots on the prepared cookie sheet, drizzle with oil, season with salt and pepper, and toss to coat. Spread the carrots in a single layer, without touching. Roast, stirring once about halfway through, until fork-tender, about 15 minutes. Ask an adult to help you remove the cookie sheet from the oven and set aside.

Combine the quinoa and 2 cups water in a saucepan. Set the pan over high heat and bring to a boil. Immediately reduce the heat to low, cover, and simmer until the water is absorbed, 15 to 20 minutes. Remove the lid and fluff the quinoa with a fork.

While the carrots and quinoa are cooking, make the vinaigrette. In a bowl, combine the orange juice, vinegar, and mustard. Pour in the oil slowly, whisking until well blended. Taste and season with salt and pepper. Set aside. Peel the oranges and divide them into sections.

In a large bowl, toss the warm quinoa with the spinach. Pour in half of the vinaigrette and toss to coat. Taste and add more dressing as needed.

To serve, mound the quinoa-spinach mixture on a platter or in individual bowls and top with the roasted carrots, orange sections, edamame, and hazelnuts. Using a vegetable peeler, shave thin pieces from the cheese over the salad. Serve right away.

Pink Orange Cake

This pretty cake has a naturally pink frosting from the juice of blood oranges. Blood oranges have a relatively short winter season, so if you don't have any, you can just stick to regular oranges, although the glaze won't have the same pink hue.

MAKES ABOUT 8 SERVINGS

CAKE

1½ cups all-purpose flour

½ teaspoon baking powder

3 large eggs

¼ cup fresh orange juice

1 teaspoon pure vanilla extract

1 cup granulated sugar

¾ cup (1½ sticks) unsalted butter, at room temperature

Grated zest of 2 oranges

½ teaspoon salt

(See additional ingredients, next page)

 Preheat the oven to 350°F. Generously butter a 9-by-5-inch loaf pan, then line it with a piece of parchment paper, extending it up and over the sides.

To make the cake, in a small bowl, whisk together the flour and baking powder. In a glass measuring pitcher, whisk together the eggs, orange juice, and vanilla.

In a large bowl, using an electric mixer, beat the granulated sugar, butter, orange zest, and salt on medium-high speed until fluffy and pale, about 3 minutes. Turn off the mixer and scrape down the bowl with a rubber spatula. Add the egg mixture, a third of it at a time, and beat until well blended (the mixture will look a little curdled but this is okay). Turn off the mixer. Add the flour mixture, half of it at a time, and beat until just combined. Do not overmix. Give the batter a final stir with a rubber spatula to make sure it is fully combined.

~ *Continued on page 126* ~

Juicy how-to

Be sure to zest your oranges before juicing them. It's really hard to zest squishy orange peels!

GLAZE

1 cup powdered sugar

1 tablespoon plus ½ teaspoon fresh blood orange juice or orange juice, plus more as needed

About 4 very thin slices blood orange, seeded, or a handful of edible flowers (optional)

~ *Continued from page 125* ~

Pour the batter into the prepared pan and spread the top evenly.

Bake until the top of the cake is golden brown and a wooden skewer inserted into the center comes out clean, about 65 minutes. If the cake browns too quickly, cover the top with aluminum foil after about 45 minutes. Remove the loaf pan from the oven and set atop a wire rack. Let cool in the pan for about 10 minutes, then, using the parchment, carefully lift the cake out of the pan. Remove the parchment and place the cake on the rack. Let cool completely.

To make the glaze, sift the powdered sugar into a bowl. Add the blood orange juice and whisk until smooth. It should be thick but fall in ribbons from the spoon; if it's too thick, add a few drops more juice, but be careful a not to add too much at once. Using a large spoon, drizzle the glaze over the top of the cake, allowing it to drip down the sides. Let stand for 2 minutes to set, then lay the blood orange slices or edible flowers (if using) decoratively over the top. Cut the cake into thick slices and serve right away.

Creamy Citrus Ice Pops

Here are two ways to create tangy-creamy ice pops, a refreshingly good-for-you treat to beat the heat in the summertime. Because there are lots of fun—and differently sized—pop molds out there, you may end up with more or fewer than this recipe yields.

MAKES 6 POPS PER FLAVOR

ORANGE-STRAWBERRY POPS

1 cup sliced strawberries

2 teaspoons plus 1 tablespoon agave nectar, or to taste

¾ cup whole-milk vanilla yogurt

¼ cup fresh orange juice

¼ teaspoon grated orange zest

(See additional ingredients, next page)

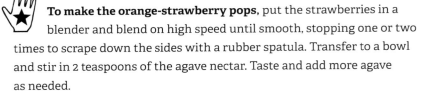

To make the orange-strawberry pops, put the strawberries in a blender and blend on high speed until smooth, stopping one or two times to scrape down the sides with a rubber spatula. Transfer to a bowl and stir in 2 teaspoons of the agave nectar. Taste and add more agave as needed.

In a second bowl, stir together the yogurt, orange juice, orange zest, and the remaining 1 tablespoon agave nectar until combined.

Set up your pop molds in the stand, then spoon a little strawberry purée and then a little orange-yogurt mixture into the molds, alternating between the two mixtures and dividing them evenly between the molds. Leave about a ¾-inch space at the top. Using a wooden skewer, swirl the mixture a little up the sides of the molds to create pretty patterns. Add a little more purée if needed so that the mixture comes to ½ inch below the top of the mold. Attach the tops and sticks.

Freeze for at least 4 hours, or until the pops are frozen solid. To remove the pops from the mold, dip the mold in a bowl of warm water, then slide the mold off the pop. Serve right away.

~ *Continued on page 128* ~

Sweet swirls
The swirls of strawberry purée add color, but you can omit the purée and make classic creamy pops by doubling the yogurt-citrus mixture.

~ *Continued from page 127* ~

To make the strawberry lemonade pops, put the strawberries in a blender and blend on high speed until smooth, stopping one or two times to scrape down the sides with a rubber spatula. Transfer to a bowl and stir in 2 teaspoons of the agave nectar. Taste and add more agave as needed.

STRAWBERRY LEMONADE POPS

1 cup sliced strawberries

2 teaspoons plus 2 tablespoons agave nectar, or to taste

1 cup whole-milk vanilla yogurt

2 tablespoons fresh lemon juice

¼ teaspoon grated lemon zest

In a second bowl, stir together the yogurt, lemon juice, lemon zest, and the remaining 2 tablespoons agave nectar until combined.

Set up your pop molds in the stand, then spoon a little lemon-yogurt mixture into the molds, followed by a little strawberry purée, and then a little lemon-yogurt mixture, dividing them evenly between the molds. Leave about a 1/2-inch space at the top. Attach the tops and sticks.

Freeze for at least 4 hours, or until the pops are frozen solid. To remove the pops from the mold, dip the mold in a bowl of warm water, then slide the mold off the pop. Serve right away.

Lemon Tart with Raspberries

Lemons are great to bake with because their tart flavor keeps desserts from becoming overly sweet. Soft cream cheese, delicate raspberries, and a crunchy graham cracker crust make the perfect texture combo for every bite.

MAKES 8 SERVINGS

2 large eggs

⅔ cup granulated sugar

12 ounces cream cheese, at room temperature

½ cup sour cream

2 tablespoons all-purpose flour

2 teaspoons grated lemon zest

Juice from 1 lemon

1 teaspoon pure vanilla extract

1 store-bought 9-inch graham cracker crust

6 ounces raspberries

Powdered sugar, for dusting

 Preheat the oven to 350°F.

Combine the eggs and granulated sugar in a food processor and process until smooth. Add the cream cheese, pulse a few times to break it up, and then process until smooth. Add the sour cream, flour, lemon zest, lemon juice, and vanilla and process just until smooth. Pour the filling into the crust and spread the top evenly.

Bake until the top looks firm and is set when you gently shake the pan, 35 to 45 minutes. Remove the pan from the oven and set it atop a wire rack. Let cool for about 1 hour. Cover with plastic wrap and refrigerate until cold, at least 3 hours or up to overnight. Spoon the raspberries on top of the tart and dust with powdered sugar just before serving. Cut into wedges and serve cold.

Pretty presentation
After baking, place the tart in a fancy pie plate to hide the aluminum shell of the store-bought crust.

Sparkling Limeade

This limeade is delicious as is, or can be used as a base for many types of drinks by adding other fruits, such as strawberries, raspberries, cherries, and tropical fruit. Kaffir lime leaves are popular in Asian cuisines; if you can't find them, leave them out.

MAKES 4 SERVINGS

SIMPLE SYRUP

1 cup sugar

1½ cups water

12 limes

Ice cubes

About 8 lime slices

8 Kaffir lime leaves

1 liter sparkling water

To make the simple syrup, combine the sugar and water in a small saucepan. Set the pan over medium heat and bring to a boil. Immediately reduce the heat to medium-low and simmer until the sugar has completely dissolved, stirring once or twice, about 10 minutes. Remove from the heat and let cool in the pan (careful, the syrup will be very hot).

Using a citrus zester or Microplane, grate the zest of 4 of the limes and set aside. Cut all the limes in half and use a handheld juicer to juice the halves.

Fill a pitcher with ice and pour in the cooled simple syrup and the juice. Add the zest, lime slices, and Kaffir lime leaves and stir. Top with sparkling water. Pour the limeade into 4 ice-filled glasses and serve right away.

Pink Grapefruit Granita

Granita is crushed, flavored ice. You can use any type of grapefruit for this recipe, but pink grapefruit will make it a really pretty color. Squeeze your own grapefruit juice or buy it fresh, and be sure to leave enough time for chilling the syrup and freezing the ice.

MAKES 4 TO 6 SERVINGS

¾ cup sugar

2 teaspoons grated grapefruit zest

1½ cups unsweetened grapefruit juice

In a small saucepan, stir together the sugar, ¾ cup water, and the grapefruit zest. Set over medium-high heat and bring to a boil. Continue to boil, stirring frequently, until the syrup is clear with no visible grains of sugar, 1 to 2 minutes. Remove from the heat, pour into a bowl, and let cool to room temperature, about 20 minutes. Cover the bowl with plastic wrap and refrigerate until the syrup is very cold, about 1 hour.

Pour the chilled grapefruit syrup through a fine-mesh sieve into a bowl to strain out the zest, pressing hard on the zest with the back of a spoon to extract as much flavor as possible. Add the grapefruit juice and stir well.

Pour the mixture into a shallow metal baking pan. Place in the freezer and freeze, whisking every 30 minutes, until semi-firm, about 3 hours. Cover with plastic wrap and return to the freezer without stirring until frozen solid, at least 8 hours or up to 24 hours.

At least 1 hour before serving, place 4 glasses in the freezer. To serve, using a fork, scrape the surface of the granita into fine ice crystals. Scoop the granita into the frozen glasses. Serve right away.

Index

Weldon Owen is a division of Bonnier Publishing USA

1045 Sansome Street, Suite 100, San Francisco, CA 94111
www.weldonowen.com

WELDON OWEN, INC.
President & Publisher Roger Shaw
SVP, Sales & Marketing Amy Kaneko

Associate Publisher Amy Marr
Project Editor Alexis Mersel

Creative Director Kelly Booth
Associate Art Director Lisa Berman
Original Design Alexandra Zeigler

Production Director Michelle Duggan
Imaging Manager Don Hill

Photographer Nicole Hill Gerulat
Food Stylist Lillian Kang
Wardrobe & Prop Stylists Ethel Brennan, Veronica Olson
Hair & Makeup Kathy Hill

AMERICAN GIRL *GARDEN TO TABLE*
Conceived and produced by Weldon Owen, Inc.
In collaboration with Williams Sonoma, Inc.
3250 Van Ness Avenue, San Francisco, CA 94109

Printed and bound in China

First printed in 2018
10 9 8 7 6 5 4 3 2 1

Library of Congress Cataloging in Publication
data is available

ISBN: 978-1-68188-360-1

ACKNOWLEDGMENTS
Weldon Owen wishes to thank the following people for their generous support to help produce this book:
Erica Allen, Matt Araquistain, Sadie Bowler, Bonnie Hughes, Jane Tunks Demel, Lexi Hager,
Josephine Hsu, Kevin Kunishi, Kim Laidlaw, Veronica Laramie, Rachel Markowitz, Taylor Olson,
Elizabeth Parson, Tamara White, Nadya Dabyki/Shutterstock: page 125

A VERY SPECIAL THANK YOU TO:
Our models: Kailey Bridston, Kristina Buttner, Serra Denayer, Jasmine Elrabadi, Eden Fronckowiak,
Avenlie Fullmer, Cole Gerulat, Evie Gerulat, Harlan Groetchen, Rue Holden, Milan Hoy,
Ryann Jensen, Condoleeza Krutsch, Cailey Quita, Piper Vandersluis, Celai West

Our locations: McBride Briar Patch, Mitchell Farms, Chip Hutchinson's Pumpkin Patch,
South Coast Farms, The Hulme Family

Our party resources: Rice by Rice

Collect Them All

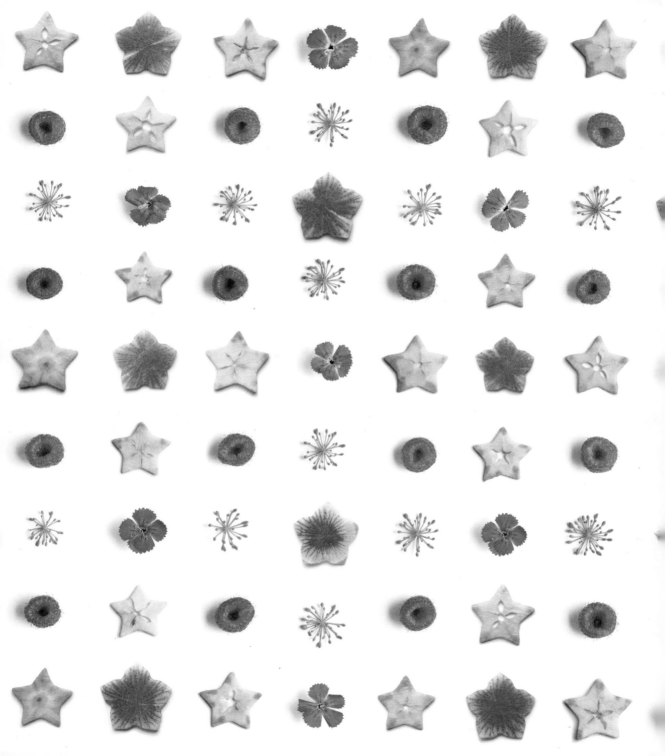